LAW OF AGENCY

Professor Richard Stone, LLB, LLM
Department of Law
Nottingham Trent University

Cavendish
Publishing
Limited

First published in Great Britain 1996 by Cavendish Publishing Limited, The Glass House, Wharton Street, London WC1X 9PX
Telephone: 0171-278 8000   Facsimile: 0171-278 8080

British Library Cataloguing in Publication Data

Stone, Richard
Law of Agency
I Title
344.20629

ISBN 1 874241 87 2

Printed and bound in Great Britain

PREFACE

The law of agency is an important concept in modern law, most obviously in the commercial sphere, but also in other areas. It deals with the various situations where one person is deemed by the law to be acting on behalf of another, whether by their intention or otherwise. The purpose of this book is to provide a guide to the main principles of English law which govern relationships of this kind. One of the objectives has been to provide this guidance within a manageable scope, so that the student, academic, or practitioner, can see the outline of a particular area, and the issues which it raises, without necessarily having to cope with its detail. For those who wish to investigate further, they may well pursue their researches through one of the two classic works on the topic currently available, ie *Bowstead on Agency*, the undisputed 'bible' of the subject (currently in its 15th edition and under the editorship of Dr Francis Reynolds), or (almost as valuable) Professor G Fridman's *Law of Agency* (6th edition). Any writer on agency must acknowledge the debt owed to these two works, and the reader of this book will find that they are referred to extensively in both footnotes and text.

Agency is not an area of law which develops with great rapidity, but there has been a regular flow of case law in recent years, particularly on the issue of 'authority'. This is, of course, given detailed consideration. In addition there has been a major development in relation to 'commercial agents' as a result of the implementation of the European Directive 86/653/EEC by the Commercial Agents (Council Directive) Regulations 1993, which came into force on the 1 January 1994. Various aspects of these regulations are discussed at length in Chapters 1, 3, and 6. The decision has been taken to deal with the effect of the regulations in separate sections within these chapters (with appropriate cross-references), rather than attempting to integrate discussion alongside the relevant common law principles. Time may show that the existence of the regulations has an effect on the common law as well, and any subsequent edition of this book may require a review of this decision, but currently it is felt that it is more satisfactory to deal with this new regime, which relates to one type of fairly narrowly defined agent, as a separate and largely self-contained area.

I must acknowledge here the patience of the editorial staff at Cavendish, and in particular Jo Reddy and Kate Nicol, in waiting for the delivery of the manuscript. In addition, I would like to thank my eldest daughter, Miranda, for making sure that I did not forget my obligation to complete it.

The law is stated as far as possible as it stood on 1 December 1995.

Richard Stone
Oadby
December 1995

CONTENTS

TABLE OF CASES

C

D

E

M

N

O

P

Q

R

TABLE OF STATUTES

CHAPTER 1

THE NATURE OF AGENCY

INTRODUCTION

Before considering the details of the legal rules which govern the concept of agency in English law, it is necessary to discuss the nature of the concept itself. Although it is a practical and useful concept, it is not easy to pin down or define. Moreover, it is used to cover a wide range of situations and may at times become confused with other legal concepts. There are also some special types of agency with particular characteristics which need to be noted.

This chapter deals with the following general issues by way of introduction to the more detailed discussion of the legal rules and principles contained in Chapters 2–6:

- the role of agency;
- the definition of agency;
- the distinction of agency from other legal relationships;
- the different types of agent.

THE ROLE OF AGENCY

The role for a concept of agency, under which one person is empowered to act on behalf of another, appears most obviously in the commercial field. The complex relationships of the modern business world, stretching across continents, could not possibly be managed if every deal had to be made in person. Even within the context of everyday life, however, the concept has an important role to play. The owner of the corner shop does not expect to deal directly with every customer who wants to buy something. A shop assistant may well be employed to handle transactions and will in some respects be acting as an agent. The intermediary, or agent, thus enables business at all levels to be conducted much more smoothly and efficiently. Indeed, in some situations business would be impossible without such a person. For example, once the law has recognised the idea of the corporate personality, the existence of a 'company' as a legal person distinct from any human being, the agent becomes essential. A company cannot act other than through the human beings who organise its affairs – for example, its directors. They are not in these circumstances the company: they simply act in the company's name. They are its 'agents'.

Given the obvious practical utility of the concept of an 'agent', and the relatively straightforward notion of one person acting on behalf of another, why does it require lengthy explanation and analysis? There are a number of reasons. First, it is not easy to isolate precisely what are the characteristics which identify someone as an agent. These problems are considered later in this chapter and in Chapter 2. Second, many problems arise as to the limits of an agent's authority, both in respect of the person for whom the agent is acting, and as regards those who deal with the agent. Discussion of these and related issues will appear in Chapters 3, 4 and 5. Third, agency will often give rise to a conflict with one of the basic doctrines of the English law of contract, ie the doctrine of privity. Its role as a means of diluting the effects of the doctrine of privity is considered here.

Agency and privity

The doctrine of privity of contract states that no one who is not a party to a contract can have rights or liabilities under it.[1] The whole basis of agency, as it applies to contracts, however, is that the two people who negotiate the deal are not the people brought into a contractual relationship. Once the contract is made, the agent normally drops out, leaving the person on whose behalf the agent was negotiating to step in as the contracting party. It may be objected that the person dealing with the agent knows all along that they are really going to be contracting with someone else, and so this is not a true exception to the privity doctrine. In some situations, however, the law of agency will allow the agent to act as if the contract is being made on the agent's behalf: only when the contract is concluded is the true contractor revealed. This aspect of agency, known as the doctrine of the 'undisclosed principal',[2] does operate against the doctrine of privity, but is accepted because of its usefulness in commercial contexts where it may be undesirable or unnecessary for the existence or identity of the contractor to be revealed until the contract is made.

The existence of agency can also at times be used by the courts as a way round the restrictions of the doctrine of privity. One of the most

---

[1] See eg *Tweddle v Atkinson* (1861) 1 B & S 393; Treitel, *The Law of Contract*, 9th edn, Ch 15; Cheshire, Fifoot and Furmston, *Law of Contract*, 12th edn, Ch 14; Stone, *Contract Law*, Ch 4.

[2] It is discussed in more detail below, at p 93.

obvious examples of this arose in the case of *The Eurymedon*.[3] A contract for the carriage of goods by sea purported to give the benefit of an exemption clause to the stevedores who were to unload the goods. The stevedores were not parties to the carriage contract. The Privy Council, however, was prepared to find that the carriers had acted as agents in making a unilateral contract on behalf of the stevedores, under which the owners of the goods promised the benefit of the exemption clause in return for the stevedores' unloading of the goods. This use of the concept of agency is clearly artificial, in that it is hard to believe that those who were involved in the transactions ever thought about them in the terms suggested by the Privy Council. On the other hand, it is in line with the general principle of using agency to help smooth the wheels of commerce, and to give practical effect to the objectives of contracting parties. The owners and the carriers had clearly intended at the time of contracting that the stevedores should have the benefit of the exemption clause. The concept of agency was simply used to circumvent the normal consequences of the doctrine of privity and achieve that aim.[4]

A similar use of the concept in a non-commercial context can be seen in relation to undue influence or misrepresentation. It is not uncommon for a person, very often a husband, to induce another (eg his wife), by undue influence or misrepresentation, to put up property as security for a loan being made to him. This results in a contract between the person influenced or misled and the lender. If the debtor defaults, can the innocent person escape the consequences of the contract, which may have put their home at risk? The general law of contract would seem to say no, because the influence or misrepresentation came not from the creditor, but from the debtor (eg the husband), who was not privy to the contract. In some cases, however, the courts have been prepared to regard the debtor as acting as agent for the creditor in obtaining the security, so that the creditor is infected with the debtor's wrongdoing. This approach was taken in *Kings North Trust Ltd v Bell*,[5] where a husband was entrusted by the creditor to obtain his wife's signature to a mortgage deed. It was also recognised as a possibility in *Coldunell v Gallon*,[6] and *Barclays Bank plc v Kennedy*.[7] Although the House of Lords, in *Barclays Bank v O'Brien*,[8] has now categorised the use of an agency

---

3   [1975] AC 154, [1974] 1 All ER 1015.
4   *Cf* also *The New York Star* [1980] 3 All ER 257.
5   [1986] 1 WLR 119.
6   [1986] 1 QB 1184.
7   (1988) 21 HLR 132. See also *Avon Finance Co Ltd v Bridger* [1985] 2 All ER 281.
8   [1993] 4 All ER 417.

analysis in such cases as likely to be 'artificial', it has not ruled out its use in appropriate cases.[9]

The Eurymedon and the undue influence cases illustrate the point that an agency relationship may not always be easy to spot, and that the courts may be prepared to find its existence in unusual circumstances. With this in mind, it is now time to turn to the attempt to define the concept of agency in English law.

THE DEFINITION OF AGENCY

Agency is a legal relationship under which one person (the agent) acts on behalf of another (the principal). The existence of the relationship is a matter of law, in that there is no need for the parties to intend to create a relationship of agency for one to exist, nor is the fact that they have labelled their relationship as one of agency conclusive. An example of the former point may be found in the 'avoidance of privity' cases noted in the previous section. A further example is *Heatons Transport (St Helens) Ltd v Transport and General Workers Union*,[10] where the House of Lords held that shop stewards were agents of their trade union, thus making the union responsible for their unlawful actions in an industrial dispute. It is by no means certain that this could be said to have represented the intentions of the union or its shop stewards. The lack of a need for intention appears even more clearly in relation to agency created by statute.[11]

The converse point, that a label is not conclusive, is shown by *Lamb (WT) & Sons v Goring Brick Company*.[12] The defendants were brick manufacturers who appointed the plaintiffs as 'sole selling agents' of bricks and other materials produced by the defendants. This was held by the Court of Appeal not to have created an agency relationship. The agreement between the plaintiffs and the defendants required the plaintiffs to pay the defendants for all goods received each month, at a 10% discount, whether they had sold them on or not. This was regarded as incompatible with an agency relationship, where an agent would not be expected to have such an obligation. The contract was essentially one of sale rather than agency.

If, then, it is a matter of law as to whether a relationship of agency exists, how do the courts reach a decision? What are the essential

---

9   *Ibid* at p 428.
10 [1972] 3 All ER 101; [1973] AC 15.
11 Eg Consumer Credit Act 1974, s 56. See below, Chapter 2, p 38.
12 [1932] 1 KB 710.

elements of a relationship which identify it as being one of agency? Unfortunately this is a question to which there is no easy answer, and indeed considerable disagreement among the leading authorities on the area.

The definition in the current edition of Bowstead[13] identifies two important elements:

- the fiduciary nature of the relationship;
- the consent, express or implied, of the two parties to the agent's acting on behalf of the principal.

It is true that agency does give rise to fiduciary obligations, on the part of the agent in particular. The position of agent must not, for example, be used to make a secret profit.[14] On the other hand, fiduciary obligations arise in all sorts of areas of the law without agency being involved. It is surely right to conclude, as Fridman does,[15] that such obligations are a *consequence* of the agency relationship, not an identifying feature. *the same thing !*

Bowstead's other factor, ie consent, is also inadequate as a determinant of the existence of agency. Agency can arise without either party wishing to create such a relationship. This is not inevitably inconsistent with Bowstead's position, since it could be argued that in a case like *Heatons v TGWU*,[16] although the parties have not realised that they have consented to a relationship which the courts regard as one of agency, there was nevertheless consent. Some established categories of agency are, however, more difficult to fit within the consent model. *consent implied by courts* Agency by estoppel, agency of necessity, agency by statute, all arise without the need for consent. Bowstead recognises this, but maintains that the consent model is the *paradigm* of the agency relationship and has value for that reason:

> it is from their similarity in various respects to this situation that the others derive their legal force.[17]

Although there are judicial statements which can be found in support of this position,[18] there are others which clearly do not accept

---

13 *Bowstead on Agency*, 15th edn, 1985 (hereinafter cited simply as 'Bowstead'), Article 1, p 1.
14 This is dealt with in more detail in Chapter 3.
15 *Law of Agency*, 6th edn, 1990, p 11.
16 [1972] 3 All ER 101; [1973] AC 15.
17 Bowstead, p 4.
18 Eg Lord Cranworth in *Pole v Leask* (1863) 33 LJCh 155, at p 161; Lord Pearson in *Garnac Grain Co Inc v HMF Faure & Fairclough Ltd* [1968] AC 1130n, 1137.

it,[19] and it is difficult to see that it does actually accord with the reality of how agency is found to exist. Why should a definition which specifies consent as an essential element be found to include situations which do not involve consent on the basis that they are 'derivatives' from the paradigm?[20] Such an approach could have dramatic consequences for the expansion of the law of contract if it were to be applied generally to that area.

Fridman's definition of agency takes a different approach. For him, the essence of the relationship lies in the ability of the agent:

> to affect the principal's legal position in respect of strangers to the relationship by the making of contracts or the disposition of property.[21]

Thus the agent exercises *power* which gives rise to a *liability* on the part of the principal. The analysis of agency in terms of a power/liability relationship may be traced back at least as far as Hohfeld, in his classic work of analytical jurisprudence, *Some Fundamental Legal Conceptions as Applied in Judicial Reasoning*.[22] In trying to unpack the concept of the legal 'right', Hohfeld argued that the 'right' of an agent to act on behalf of their principal was in fact a 'power' possessed by the agent, which gave rise to a correlative 'liability' on the part of the principal.[23] The approach has also been adopted by Dowrick,[24] and by Markesinis and Munday.[25]

This analysis places the emphasis on the power given by the relationship, rather than the elements which identify it. For that reason it may be felt to be not particularly helpful as a definition. A court using Fridman's approach would have to consider the legal consequences of a relationship as the basis for deciding if it was one of agency: X is acting for Y, and has the power to dispose of Y's property, and therefore X is an agent. One would expect a definition to operate the other way round: X has the characteristics of an agent acting for Y, and therefore X has the power to dispose of Y's property.

The definition also suffers from a similar defect to that put forward by Bowstead, in that it is not comprehensive. Not all agents have the

---

19 Eg Lord Wilberforce in *Branwhite v Worcester Works Finance Ltd* [1968] 3 All ER 104, at p 122.
20 Bowstead, p 4.
21 Fridman, p 9.
22 (1913) 23 *Yale Law Journal* 16; references here are to the reprint in *Fundamental Legal Conceptions*, Yale University Press, 1919, p 23.
23 *Ibid*, p 52.
24 *The Relationship of Principal and Agent* (1954) 17 MLR 24.
25 *An Outline of the Law of Agency*, 3rd edn, 1992, p 8.

power to affect their principal's legal position in the way suggested, the most obvious exception being the estate agent.[26] Such an agent will not generally have the power to make a binding contract on behalf of the principal, nor to dispose of the principal's property. Fridman's answer is to class the estate agent as 'anomalous',[27] but this is hardly satisfactory in relation to such a common type of agency. It is not clear why supporters of this analysis feel the need to limit the legal relationships affected to the two named, ie making contracts, and disposing of property. An estate agent, for example, may be delegated the authority to show someone round a house, or to give them the keys to enable them to do so. Here the agent is given the power to grant a licence to enter property, which would normally be the prerogative of the property owner. In other words, the agent is assuming legal powers of the principal, but not necessarily those relating to the making of contracts, or the disposal of interests in property. There is also the possibility that the agent who acts tortiously or criminally will make the principal vicariously liable.[28] If the power/liability analysis is to be used, therefore, it would seem preferable to put it on a broader basis, and include within its scope all the ways in which an agent may affect the legal position of their principal, rather than limiting it to contracts and the disposal of property.

In the end a comprehensive definition may be impossible and perhaps unnecessary.[29] The essence of agency seems, however, to concern the acquisition of legal authority by the agent. This may come from the consent of the principal, or it may arise in other ways. Agency exists as a matter of law where a third party is entitled to assume that the agent has authority to do what they are doing, even though the agent is in fact acting on behalf of someone else, whether or not the third party is aware that this is the case. The actions of the agent will then affect the legal position of the principal.

THE DISTINCTION OF AGENCY FROM OTHER LEGAL RELATIONSHIPS

Because of the difficulty identified above in trying to formulate a comprehensive definition of agency, it is important that at least the boundaries between agency and other legal relationships or concepts should be clear. In particular it is important to distinguish between

---

26 See Bridge (1977) 14 JSPTL 150.
27 Fridman, p 10.
28 See below, Chapter 4, p 111-126.
29 See eg Markesinis and Munday, *op cit*, p 1.

agency on the one hand, and sale, trusts, and employment on the other. The relationship between agency and bailment will also be briefly considered.

Sale

The fact that an agent will commonly have the power to sell the principal's property means that it is important to distinguish the agency aspects of the relationship from the sale itself. It is not true to say that in every situation where X puts goods into the hands of Y with a view to their being sold to Z there is therefore a relationship of agency between X and Y. We have already seen one example of this in the case of *Lamb v Goring Brick Co.*[30] As in that case, the problem tends to arise where Y is said to be the exclusive or sole 'agent' for the sale of X's goods. To decide whether the relationship is truly one of agency it is necessary to look in particular at the arrangements for payment. Clearly if, Y, the so-called agent, is under an obligation to pay for goods put into Y's hands irrespective of whether they have been sold on or not, the arrangement is not one of agency.[31] Even where there is no such obligation, there may be no agency if the price at which goods are to be sold is determined by Y rather than X, particularly if Y is to keep any profit on the transaction. The making of such an independent profit will normally be regarded as inconsistent with agency.[32] In *Customs & Excise Commissioners v Paget*,[33] the question was whether a school was acting as agent for a photographer in selling photographs of its pupils to their parents. Otton J noted that the VAT tribunal had considered whether the school was taking commission, and had concluded that:

> the school was making a profit from the resale. In rejecting the idea of commission the value added tax tribunal has concluded that the school is selling in its own right and has rejected one of the fundamental indicia of agency.[34]

On the other hand, the fixing of a price by X will not necessarily mean that Y is an agent.[35] In the end, each case must be decided in the light of all the facts, and the extent to which Y is under the control of, and accountable to, X. What is clear is that agency and sale are mutually exclusive. Y, the buyer, cannot at the same time be an agent; Y, the agent,

---

30 [1932] 1 KB 710. Above, p 4.
31 *Ibid.*
32 See below, Chapter 3, p 61.
33 [1989] STC 773
34 *Ibid*, at p 782.
35 *Michelin Tyre Co Ltd v Mc Farlane (Glasgow) Ltd* (1917) 55 Sc L Rep 35.

will obtain no ownership rights over goods put into his possession by X with a view to sale.[36]

Trust

There are similarities between agency and trust, in that both agents and trustees have control over property to which other people are beneficially entitled. Moreover, agency involves fiduciary duties not unlike those attaching to trusteeship.[37] And both concepts can be used as a means of defeating or circumventing the doctrine of privity.[38] There are, however, significant differences.

First, there are differences in the nature of the interests in the property which is subject to a trust or is dealt with by an agent. A trustee has a legal interest in such property, whereas an agent has no property interest at all. The beneficiary of a trust, on the other hand, on whose behalf the trustee acts, has only an equitable interest, while the principal, on whose behalf the agent acts, has a legal interest.

Second, there are differences in the duties and responsibilities of those involved. A beneficiary, for example, is not responsible for the acts of a trustee who acts fraudulently. The fraudulent agent, however, may well bring liability on the principal. The trustee, on the other hand, has positive duties to act, which may well be of a general nature, whereas the agent is more generally given powers rather than duties, with specific obligations arising only from particular transactions.

These differences are not mutually exclusive, however. A trustee may act as an agent in some circumstances, and an agent's fiduciary duties are at times very similar to those of a trustee.[39] The distinctions noted above are perhaps clearer in the context of contractual obligations, as opposed to those arising in tort.[40]

Employment

Confusion can arise here from the fact that we may talk of a principal *employing* an agent. And, as we shall see,[41] a principal will in some

---

[36] This does not preclude an agent who sells without authorisation from passing good title to an innocent third party, under the exception to the *nemo dat* rule: Sale of Goods Act 1979, s 21.

[37] See below, Chapter 3, p 60.

[38] For the use of the trust to achieve this, see eg, *Les Affréteurs Réunis SA v Walford* [1919] AC 801; *Re Flavell* (1883) Ch D 89.

[39] Bowstead, p 17.

[40] For further discussion of the relationship between agency and trusts, see Fridman, pp 20–3.

[41] See below, Chapter 3, p 111.

circumstances be vicariously liable for an agent's tortious acts, in the same way as an employer is responsible for an employee. The analogy is closest, however, in the area of tort. In contract, only an agent has the power to make contracts and dispose of the principal's property: the status of employee or independent contractor carries no such powers. This is not to deny that some employees act as agents. Shop assistants, for example, sell goods on behalf of their employers, and in doing so act as agents. Similarly, directors may be employees and at the same time act as agents for the company employing them. It is submitted, however, that the best analysis of such situations is to say that the individuals concerned are acting in a dual capacity, ie both as employees and agents. The controversy as to the exact relationship between the two statuses, dismissed by Bowstead as 'somewhat sterile',[42] perhaps simply serves to emphasise that agency is a relationship, not a post. The fact that an employee (or a trustee) is seen to be doing things which an agent can do does not mean there is no distinction between them. In law, to say that someone is an agent is not to describe the holder of an office, but to describe a person's position in a legal relationship. This relationship is not necessarily exclusive.[43] There is therefore nothing inconsistent with saying that a person can be at the same time both an employee and an agent, or an employer and a principal.

Bailment

A bailee holds goods on behalf of the bailor, under instructions as to how they are to be dealt with. Thus far there may be an overlap with agency. But a bailee has no automatic power to affect the bailor's legal relationship with third parties. The duty of the bailee may be simply to hold the goods, and return them to the bailor on request. The fact of possession may in some circumstances give rise to an 'apparent authority'.[44] Or the bailor may instruct the bailee to sell or otherwise dispose of the goods on behalf of the bailor. In such situations the bailee may become an agent. But this is best regarded in the same way as employment, ie that the individual concerned has dual status in such circumstances, both as agent and bailee.

---

42 Bowstead, p 18. More detailed discussion appears in Fridman, pp 26–32.
43 Though note the comments re sale and agency, above, p 8.
44 This concept is discussed in detail below, p 98.

THE DIFFERENT TYPES OF AGENT

In certain situations a particular label may be attached to an agent which may have some significance as to the extent or nature of the agent's powers or duties. Not all these labels are of much practical utility,[45] but they are worth noting if only because they are used in the cases, and can help in the understanding of some authorities, particularly those from the 19th century.

General or special agent

A distinction is sometimes drawn between the 'general' or 'special' agent. The general agent is engaged to carry out transactions which fall within a general area, normally of a particular trade or business. A 'managing director' will almost certainly be a 'general agent' in relation to the company, with the power to make a wide range of contracts on its behalf. Similarly, a partner may well be in the same position as regards the partnership. Outside these situations, a person may be appointed with authority, for example, to buy and sell goods generally on behalf of a principal, and thus be a general agent. By contrast, an agent may be appointed for a particular transaction, and have no authority beyond that. The agency will then cease as soon as this transaction is completed.

Although this distinction can clearly be made, and appears in some authorities, there seems to be little practical use to it.[46] To the extent that it points out a difference in the power of the agent to bind a principal, the concepts of apparent or usual authority[47] perform this role more clearly in modern cases. The fact that someone is either a special or general agent is really only of significance to the extent that it is one factor indicating to the world the limitations of the agent's authority.

Canvassing agent

There are difficulties in trying to fit estate agents within the general definition of agency, because of their severely limited authority in terms of binding their principals. Their main role is simply to find prospective customers and make the relevant introductions. If this leads to a sale, then the agent will generally be entitled to commission.[48] Some

---

[45] Though at one time they may have been.

[46] See the comments to this effect by Bowstead, at p 24, and Fridman, at p 35.

[47] See below, pp 98–110.

[48] The entitlement to commission is discussed further below, in Chapter 3, p 72.

commentators conclude that the estate agent is simply a type of 'canvassing' or 'introducing' agent, and as such an example of 'incomplete agency'.[49] Bowstead argues that whether you treat such people as agents or not depends on whether your definition of agency concentrates on the relationship between principal and agent, or the power of the agent to affect the principal's legal position. Bowstead's definition places the emphasis on the former, and so has no difficulty including the canvasser within the scope of agency. However, the view taken here is that, even adopting the approach based on the powers of the agent, the estate agent can be brought within the scope of the definition. Other 'canvassers' or 'introducers' may be more difficult to cater for, and for the purposes of this book a person who simply finds customers for another is not regarded as a true agent. There must at least be the potential for affecting the principal's legal position in some way (not necessarily contractual) for agency to arise. That is not to deny that in some situations the canvasser may not have obligations analogous to those of an agent. It is submitted, however, that they should be regarded at best as a sub-category attached to that of agency and not fully within the scope of the concept.

Mercantile agent

The Factors Act 1889, s 1(1) defines a mercantile agent as a person:

> having in the customary course of his business as such agent authority to sell goods or consign goods for the purpose of sale, or to buy goods, or to raise money on the security of goods.

This definition encompasses two types of agent recognised by the common law: factors, and brokers.

Factors

The characteristic of the factor, which distinguishes such a person from other types of mercantile agent, is that a factor is given possession of goods which are to be sold. This might arise, for example, where goods are sent by the seller from abroad. Moreover, a factor may sell in his own name, ie on behalf of an undisclosed principal.[50] The term is not, however, in common use in this sense today,[51] though the case law establishing the definition of the concept is still valid.[52]

---

49 See eg Bowstead, p 11.

50 *Baring v Corrie* (1818) 2 B&A 137.

51 As Bowstead points out, *op cit*, p 25.

52 Ie *Baring v Corrie* above, n 50; *Stevens v Biller* (1883) 25 Ch D 31. See also Fridman, pp 35–36.

Broker

A broker may well come within the definition of a 'mercantile agent', but will differ from a factor in two ways. First, a broker is not given possession of goods, and second, brokers never sell in their own name. The broker, much more so than the factor, is thus a 'facilitator' rather than a primary party. The broker negotiates, and brings buyer and seller together, but always does so clearly as a third party to the transaction. As Fridman points out, the term broker is also applied to agents who are not 'mercantile agents', such as stockbrokers, insurance brokers, or credit-brokers.

Note also the new statutory definition of a 'commercial agent', below.

Del credere agent

A *del credere* agent may also be a mercantile agent, and will often be so, since the primary use of this type of agency would appear to be transactions for the sale of goods overseas, where the principal has some doubts that the third party will pay. The *del credere* agent, in return for an increased commission, agrees to indemnify the principal if the third party defaults.[53] Many transactions where this concern arises will nowadays be dealt with by means of documentary credits or credit guarantees, but it seems that the *del credere* arrangement is still used on occasions.

Commercial agent

Some aspects of English law relating to agency have now been affected by attempts by the European Community to co-ordinate the laws of Member States. Council Directive 86/653/EEC deals with certain rights and duties of self-employed commercial agents. This Directive has been implemented in English law by means of the Commercial Agents (Council Directive) Regulations 1993.[54] which came into force on 1 January 1994. The substantive provisions of the Regulations will be noted at the relevant points in later chapters. At this stage, it is necessary to note the definition of 'commercial agent', which substantially determines the scope of the Regulations.

Regulation 2(1) defines a commercial agent for the purposes of the Regulations as:

---

[53] *Morris v Cleasby* (1816) 4 M&S 566.
[54] SI 1993/3053.

a self-employed intermediary who has continuing authority to negotiate the sale or purchase of goods on behalf of another person (the "principal"), or to negotiate and conclude the sale or purchase of goods on behalf of and in the name of that principal.

This definition indicates a fairly narrow scope for the regulations. The requirement of 'self-employment' means that any person who is an employee as well as an agent is excluded (shop assistants, for example, are thus outside the definition). Moreover, there are specific exclusions applying to officers of 'a company or association',[55] partners acting on behalf of a partnership,[56] and insolvency practitioners.[57] Company directors and receivers are not covered. The regulations are aimed simply at the independent agent, who has no other legal relationship with the principal.

To be a commercial agent the agent must have authority to negotiate for the buying and selling of goods. The authority must be 'continuing', which means that the agent appointed to deal with a particular transaction is not affected by the regulations. The agent apparently does not have to have authority to conclude contracts in order to be a commercial agent: the power to negotiate is sufficient. The wording of reg 2(1) is not altogether clear, however. As will be noted, two alternatives are recognised. The agent either has authority simply to 'negotiate', or has authority to 'negotiate and conclude' the transaction, in relation to the sale or purchase of goods. The power to negotiate on its own may be exercised simply 'on behalf of' the principal. This will presumably include an undisclosed principal. The power to negotiate and *conclude* a contract, however, must be 'on behalf of *and in the name of*' the principal. This presumably excludes an undisclosed principal. This distinction is, as Reynolds has pointed out,[58] 'curious'. It has the effect of excluding the situation where a third party enters into a contract with an unknown principal. In practice, very few agents dealing with goods will have authority to negotiate but not to conclude a contract. Only in exceptional cases, therefore, will the regulations apply where the agent is acting for an undisclosed principal.

Although the authority to negotiate re the sale or purchase of goods is a *sine qua non* of being a commercial agent, it presumably does not matter if the agent has other authority as well. There is nothing in the regulations to exclude such an agent.

---

55 Regulation 2(1)(i).

56 Regulation 2(1)(ii).

57 As defined in s 388 of the Insolvency Act 1986, or the equivalent in any other jurisdiction: reg 2(1)(iii).

58 [1994] JBL 266. He suggests that it may be necessary to refer to civil law jurisdictions for a full understanding of what is meant by 'in the name of the principal'.

Regulation 2(2) specifically excludes from the scope of the regulations three types of agent who might fall within the definition of 'commercial agent'. These are:

- gratuitous agents;
- commercial agents when dealing on commodity exchanges or in the commodity markets; and
- Crown Agents for Overseas Governments and Administrations.[59]

Finally, the provisions of the Regulations do not apply to commercial agents whose activities as such are to be considered 'secondary'.[60] In other words, commercial agency should be the agent's primary activity. This is explained further by the Schedule to the Act, which indicates (in rather a convoluted way) that where the primary purpose of the arrangement between the agent and principal is as set out below, it will fall within the Regulations. The relevant arrangements arise where:[61]

(a) the business of the principal is the sale, or as the case may be the purchase, of goods of a particular kind; and

(b) the goods concerned are such that –

   (i) transactions are normally individually negotiated and concluded on a commercial basis, and

   (ii) procuring a transaction on one occasion is likely to lead to further transactions in those goods with that customer on future occasions, or to transactions in those goods with other customers in the same geographical area or among the same group of customers, and

   (iii) that accordingly it is in the commercial interests of the principal in developing the market in those goods to appoint a representative to such customers with a view to the representative devoting effort skill and expenditure from his own resources to that end.

These provisions emphasise, as does the reference to 'continuing authority' in reg 2(1), that the regulations are concerned with relationships which at least have the potential of developing over time. Two types of relationship which might have this characteristic are, however, by virtue of para 5 of the Schedule presumed not to be commercial agencies, unless the contrary is established. These are firstly, mail order catalogue agencies for consumer goods, and secondly, consumer credit agents.

---

[59] As set up under the Crown Agents Act 1979, or its subsidiaries.
[60] Regulation 2(4).
[61] Paragraph 2.

Paragraphs 3 and 4 give further indications of characteristics which would tend to support (para 3), or go against (para 4), the relationship being a commercial agency. In favour will be the fact that the principal is the manufacturer, distributor or importer of the goods, or that the goods are specifically identified with the principal, or that the arrangement is described as one of commercial agency. Similarly, it will be likely to be a commercial agency where the agent devotes most of his time to representation of the principal (or principals), or where the goods are only normally available through the agent. Factors which will go against its being a commercial agency will arise if promotional material is supplied direct to potential customers, or if agencies are granted without reference to existing agencies in an area or within a group, or if customers select goods for themselves and merely place their orders through the agent.

Finally, the conflict of laws provision should be noted,[62] which means that the Regulations will generally only apply to activities of commercial agents in Great Britain.[63]

The provisions defining the scope of the regulations are complex, and at times will require a fine judgment as to whether a particular activity falls within them or outside. They are likely, in the end, to touch a relatively small number of agents, but the uncertainties as to their limits clearly raise the potential for confusion and perhaps litigation.

Estate agent

It has already been noted that estate agents do not fit easily into the generally accepted definitions of 'agency', because of the fact that in general they do not have the power to bind their principals to a contract with a third party. Nevertheless, estate agents are regarded as being governed by the general rules applicable to other agents, and there is much case law concerned with them, particularly in relation to the payment of commission. In addition, there is statutory regulation of estate agency by means of the Estate Agents Act 1979, and the Property Misdescriptions Act 1991.

The 1979 Act does not define an 'estate agent', but only 'estate agency work'. This was a result of a recognition that such work could be and is carried out by a range of people and organisations, not all of whom would be properly identified as 'estate agents'. The definition of 'estate agency work' is contained in s 1(1), and means:

---

62 Regulation 1(2).
63 For more detailed discussion of this aspect of the regulations, see Reynolds [1994] JBL 260, at p 267.

things done by any person in the course of a business (including a business in which he is employed) pursuant to instructions received from another person (in this section referred to as 'the client') who wishes to dispose of or acquire an interest in land –

(a) for the purpose of, or with a view to, effecting the introduction to the client of a third person who wishes to acquire or, as the case may be, dispose of such an interest; and

(b) after such an introduction has been effected in the course of that business, for the purpose of securing the disposal or, as the case may be, the acquisition of that interest.

Excluded from this definition, however, are things done by a practising solicitor, credit broker, insurance broker, or in connection with an independent survey or valuation, or a planning application.[64] Nor does the Act apply to things done by an employee where the employer is disposing of his own interest in land; or by the person who is the recipient of mortgage income in relation to the property; or in relation to an employee (whether past, present or future), and by reason of the employment.[65]

The Act contains obligations requiring the keeping of separate client accounts, and provisions ensuring that clients' money is held on trust.[66] The agent must also give, prior to entering into a contract, specified information as to payments which clients will have to make for work carried out,[67] and disclose any personal interest.[68]

Overall supervision of the conduct of estate agency work is given to the Director General of Fair Trading. Control is exercised not by means of a licensing scheme, but through the power to issue orders prohibiting 'unfit persons' from doing estate agency work.[69] In other words, people are free to engage in estate agency work, but if they are found to be unfit to do so, as a result of, for example, being convicted of a offence involving dishonesty or violence, committing sex or race discrimination, or failing to comply with the obligations imposed by the Act itself (outlined above), the Director General may issue an order prohibiting the person from engaging in certain, or all, types of estate agency work. Failure to comply with such an order amounts to a criminal offence.[70]

In addition to these general controls, a specific criminal offence related to estate agency was created by the Property Misdescriptions Act

---

[64] Section 1(2).
[65] Section 1(3).
[66] Sections 13-14.
[67] Section 18.
[68] Section 21.
[69] Section 3.
[70] Section 3(8).

1991. Under s 1 of this Act it is an offence to make, in the course of an estate agency business,[71] a false or misleading statement about a 'prescribed matter'. The Act adopts the definition of estate agency business used in the Estate Agents Act 1979 (above).[72] A 'prescribed matter' is 'any matter relating to land which is specified in an order made by the Secretary of State.' The current order relating to this provision contains a list of 30 different categories of prescribed matter.[73] These cover virtually all matters about which an estate agent might be expected to make a representation, including such things as the address of the land, outlook, availability and proximity of services or amenities, measurements, fixtures and fittings, history of ownership and use, price and previous price, length of time on the market, council tax, length and conditions of any lease, amount of any service charge, planning permissions, and the existence of rights of way.

The Act is only concerned with 'material' falsehoods – a minor error in description will not be penalised.[74] A statement may, however, be made by pictures 'or any other method of signifying meaning' as well as by speech or writing.[75]

Liability under this provision attaches to the person carrying on the estate agency business.[76] It does not, therefore, apply to the principal who has engaged the estate agent. An employee who makes a statement may be liable personally, as well as possibly making the estate agent vicariously liable (subject to a due diligence defence).[77] The approach taken by the courts to these types of criminal liability is considered in more detail in Chapter 4.[78]

---

[71] The offence also applies to a property development business.
[72] Section 1(5)(e).
[73] Property Misdescriptions (Specified Matters) Order 1992, SI 1992/2834.
[74] Section 1(5)(a).
[75] Section 1(5)(c).
[76] Section 1(1).
[77] Section 1(2); Section 2.
[78] See pp 118–126.

CHAPTER 2

CREATION OF AGENCY

INTRODUCTION

An agency relationship is frequently the result of a contract between principal and agent. However, there are other methods by which it can be created. There are in fact four ways in which agency can arise:

- by agreement (express or implied);
- by ratification;
- by operation of law;
- by estoppel.

Only the first three categories will be covered in this chapter. Agency by estoppel creates only a limited type of agency, affecting the relationship between principal and third party, rather than between principal and agent. It can be argued to be simply an aspect of an agent's, or purported agent's, apparent authority to bind the principal. As such it has clear links with the doctrine of 'ostensible authority', which is dealt with in Chapter 4. Discussion of agency by estoppel will therefore be included in that chapter.

AGENCY BY AGREEMENT

This is the most frequent type of agency. The agreement may be express or implied. Before these two types of agreement are considered, however, some general issues related to the approach of the courts to this method of creating agency need discussion.

General attitude of the courts

The most obvious way in which agency can arise is by agreement between principal and agent. This does not necessarily have to take the form of a contract, though in many cases it will. Provided there is a clear agreement, this will generally be sufficient to create the agency. Some situations are not clear-cut, however, as when the parties have undoubtedly made an agreement, and have referred to their relationship as one of agency, but the courts regard it as something else, such as a contract for sale (as, for example, in *Lamb v Goring Brick Company*).[1] In other cases, the parties may not have used the language of agency in a situation which is in law regarded as such. The general attitude of the courts to problems such as these is shown by the judgment of Lord Pearson in *Garnac Grain Co v HMF Faure and Fairclough*.[2] He starts by saying that the relationship can only be established by the consent of the parties. This is not always true, since there are situations in which agency can arise in the absence of consent. To the extent that consent is relevant, however, it will arise 'either expressly or by implication from their words or conduct'. Furthermore:[3]

> Primarily one looks to what they said and did at the time of the alleged creation of the agency. Earlier words and conduct may afford evidence of a course of dealing in existence at that time and may be taken into account more generally as historical background. Later words and conduct may have some bearing, though likely to be less important.

The most important factors are words and conduct at the time of the alleged creation of the agency. Subsidiary factors are earlier or later words or actions. The process is therefore the objective one of establishing from what the parties have said and done whether they appear to have made an agreement, and if so what it is. Once that has been established, the court must decide whether or not as a matter of law that agreement does amount to a relationship of agency. It follows, in particular from the emphasis on actions as well as words, that an agreement creating agency can be express or implied.

Express agreement

It is necessary to say little about this, except that in general no formality is necessary. In the same way that the general law of contract requires no formalities, so the creation of agency can equally take effect by means of a verbal, unrecorded, agreement. Indeed, in many cases the agreement creating the agency will be contractual, and therefore will simply fall to be judged by the normal rules for the formation of a contract. The existence of offer, acceptance, consideration and intention, will be looked for in the normal way.[4] Even where the agreement is non-contractual, however, no formalities are normally required.

---

1 Above, p 4.
2 [1968] AC 1130.
3 *Ibid*, at p 1137.
4 See eg, Treitel *The Law of Contract*, 9th edn, Chs 2–4; Cheshire, Fifoot and Furmston, *The Law of Contract*, 12th edn, Chs 3–5; Stone, *Contract Law*, Chs 2 and 3.

In one respect, however, the rules relating to the appointment of an agent are even more relaxed than the rules for creating a contract. Certain types of contract, most notably contracts relating to the sale of land,[5] have to be made in writing. Even if the agent is to have the power to make contracts of this type, however, the appointment of the agent requires no formality. An oral agreement is quite sufficient.

The one exception to this rule arises where the agent is to have the power to execute a deed – for example, a conveyance of land. In this situation it seems that the appointment of the agent must itself be by deed, for example by the creation of a 'power of attorney'.[6] Problems may arise where the principal lacks capacity, because they are a minor, or they are mentally disturbed. The law is not very clear on these issues,[7] but the following seems to represent the position. At one point Lord Denning stated that a minor could never make a valid appointment of an agent.[8] Subsequently, however, he modified this in the following terms:

> Whenever a minor can lawfully do an act on his own behalf, so as to bind himself, he can instead appoint an agent to do it for him. Thus, if a minor can lawfully bind himself by a particular contract because it is for his benefit, he can lawfully appoint an agent to do it for him.[9]

There are, in fact, two aspects of the minor's power to appoint an agent. First there is the question of whether, if the appointment is by way of contract, that contract is enforceable by the agent against the minor. Second, there is the question of whether the minor is responsible for the agent's actions, eg in making a contract with a third party. The two questions have not, however, in practice been very carefully distinguished. As regards any contract between the principal and agent, this should surely be assessed on the basis of the normal rules relating to contractual capacity. Thus, if the appointment of the agent by a minor can be regarded as a contract for necessary services, it will be binding on the minor. Webb[10] suggests that this will occur, *inter alia*, where either the contract is 'beneficial' to the minor, or it is for the purchase of necessaries. As regards the third party, they will have legal rights and obligations *vis-à-vis* the minor, where the agent has acted with authority,

---

5   Law of Property (Miscellaneous Provisions) Act 1989, s 2(1).
6   For the formalities relating to the creation of a power of attorney, see Law of Property (Miscellaneous Provisions) Act 1989, s 1 and Sch 1.
7   The most thorough consideration of the topic remains PRH Webb, *The Capacity of an Infant to Appoint an Agent* (1955) 18 MLR 461
8   *Shephard v Cartwright* [1953] Ch 728, at 755.
9   *G v G* [1970] 2 QB 643. Lord Denning cites *Doyle v White City Stadium* [1935] 1 KB 110 as an example.
10 *Op cit*, n 7, at p 471.

and has done something which is for the minor's benefit, or is something which the minor was legally entitled to do.[11]

Turning to the situation where the incapacity results from mental disability, it should first be noted that those whose affairs are under the control of the court, by virtue of Part VII of the Mental Health Act 1983, will have no capacity to appoint an agent. In relation to those whose mental state is such that, although they are not under the control of the court, they are unable to appreciate the nature of transactions they are entering into, it seems that any contract between principal and agent should again be judged on normal contractual principles. Thus, the contract will be enforceable against the principal, unless it is proved that the agent was aware of the incapacity.[12] As regards the relationship between principal and third party, however, the balance of authority suggests that the normal rules as to capacity do not apply, and any transactions entered into will be void.[13] The mentally disordered person is thus incapable of granting authority; moreover, any authority granted by a person who subsequently becomes mentally incapacitated will cease.[14]

Implied agreement

There are two different ways in which implication may be relevant when agency is created. The relationship itself may arise from implication, or the extent of the agent's powers may be implied. In this chapter we are solely concerned with the first type of implication. The second area will be dealt with in Chapter 4 in the context of looking at the extent of an agent's authority.

The implication of an agreement to create an agency relationship will arise, as with other implied relationships, where the parties have acted in such a way towards each other that the court regards their behaviour as indicating an acceptance of such an arrangement. Here, as with other areas, the courts are not concerned with what was actually going on in the minds of the parties, but rather what a reasonable person would believe to have been going on, based on what the parties have said and done. If the reasonable explanation is that the parties have implicitly agreed that one is to act as agent for the other, then the courts will find that to be the case.

---

[11] *Ibid*, at p 472.

[12] *Imperial Loan Co v Stone* [1892] 1 QB 599, as confirmed by the Privy Council in *Hart v O'Connor* [1985] 2 All ER 880.

[13] See eg *Gibbons v Wright* (1954) CLR 423, and the other cases discussed by Bowstead, *op cit*, p 32.

[14] *Yonge v Toynbee* [1910] 1 KB 215.

An example of the kind of situation where the agency relationship itself might have to be implied arose in *White v Lucas*.[15] The defendant wished to sell his house. The plaintiffs were estate agents. The defendant was not willing to place his house with the plaintiffs, but told them that if they brought him a client who would offer 25,000 guineas he might consider the offer. The defendants introduced T, who inspected the house, but nothing came of the negotiations. Some months later, however, one of the defendant's friends managed to revive negotiations with T, and he eventually bought the house. The plaintiffs claimed commission. The defendant denied any agreement to use the plaintiffs as agents. There was clearly no express agreement, but could one be implied? The judge simply directed the jury to consider whether there was 'an employment proved by the plaintiffs of their firm as agents', and then to look at whether there were any actions by plaintiffs which led to the house being sold 'through their instrumentality'. The jury found for the defendants, but we do not know whether the plaintiffs' case fell at the first hurdle or the second. It is suggested, however, that if T had made an offer straight away there would have been little difficulty in regarding the plaintiffs as having acted as agents in negotiating the transaction. The answer is probably, therefore, that the way that the parties had acted *was* sufficient to give rise to an implied relationship of agency, but that the eventual sale was not sufficiently closely linked to the original introduction to entitle the plaintiffs to claim commission.[16]

The courts have also been prepared to imply agency where this would achieve an objective that the court considers just. The cases noted in Chapter 1[17] as examples of the courts using agency to avoid the effects of privity are instances of the courts implying agency to achieve a just result. In *The Eurymedon* (1975), for example, the Privy Council clearly thought that all the parties had intended and expected the stevedores to be able to take advantage of the exemption clause in the contract of carriage when they were unloading the goods. They were not parties to that contract, however. The court found that there was a unilateral contract, made by the carriers as agents for the stevedores, giving the stevedores the benefit of the clause in exchange for their agreement to unload the goods. No agency relationship between stevedores and carriers had been explicitly agreed, but the court clearly felt that it was acceptable to imply such a relationship on the facts of the case.

---

[15] (1887) 3 TLR 516.

[16] For further discussion of the recovery of commission by estate agents, see below, pp 72–79.

[17] Above, p 2.

In *The Eurymedon* the implication of agency had the effect of giving the third party the benefit of the contract. Again, as has been noted in Chapter 1,[18] a similar approach has been used in some cases to 'infect' a party to a contract with the wrongdoing of a person who is not a party to it. The type of situation where this has happened has been where the wrongdoer has been negotiating a loan, generally in order to support a business. The lender has wanted some security. The potential debtor cannot provide security from within their own resources, and so persuades another, by undue influence, or misrepresentation, to act as 'guarantor'. The guarantor enters into an agreement with the lender, on the basis of the debtor's undue influence or misrepresentation. Can the lender, who is unaware of the wrongdoing, enforce the guarantee against the guarantor?

In *Kings North Trust Ltd v Bell*[19] the debtor was a husband, who persuaded his wife, by means of a fraudulent misrepresentation, to sign a mortgage deed over the matrimonial home. Dillon LJ regarded this as being governed by 'the general law of principal and agent' under which:

> the principal (the creditor), however personally innocent, who instructs an agent (the husband) to achieve a particular end (the signing of the document by the wife) is liable for any fraudulent misrepresentation made by the agent in achieving that end, including any continuing misrepresentation made earlier by the agent and not corrected.[20]

It is quite clear that in such a situation the husband's agency is being implied from the actions of the parties, rather than being expressly created. Subsequently, in *Barclays Bank v O'Brien*[21] a different Court of Appeal doubted the validity of this approach, on the basis of its artificiality. The House of Lords, in the same case, however, recognised that there are situations, albeit rare, where such an analysis is valid.[22]

A similar approach, infecting the principal with the tortious acts of an implied agent, and based on the practicalities of the situation, can be seen in the House of Lords' decision in *Heatons Transport (St Helens) Ltd v Transport and General Workers Union*[23] that the union shop stewards were agents for the union.[24]

---

18 *Ibid.*

19 [1986] 1 All ER 423. A similar analysis was adopted, though not applied on the facts, in *Coldunell Ltd v Gallon* [1986] 1 All ER 429.

20 *Ibid*, at p 427.

21 Ie [1992] 4 All ER 983.

22 [1993] 4 All ER 417, *per* Lord Browne-Wilkinson, at p 428.

23 [1973] AC 15.

24 Above, p 4.

These cases show that the courts are willing to use the implication of agency in a flexible way, to achieve objectives perceived as desirable, and limited only by the rather nebulous concept of 'artificiality'. The concept is 'nebulous' because it is difficult to see, for example, that the use of agency in the husband/wife cases of undue influence or misrepresentation, is any more artificial than its use in *The Eurymedon*, or the cases that have followed it. It is true that these latter cases are concerned with a commercial context in which the concept of agency has a more obviously acceptable role, and that its use is to give effect to the clear intentions of the parties,[25] but these factors themselves, rather than the presence or absence of 'artificiality', should be used as the distinguishing features.

AGENCY BY RATIFICATION

A principal is not always going to be unhappy about the activities of a unauthorised 'agent', who has made contracts in the name of the principal. If the agent has made a good bargain, the principal may be quite happy to step in to take over the agreement. English law allows this by use of the concept of 'ratification'.

Nature of ratification

The concept of ratification allows a principal to adopt the actions of an 'agent' who has acted without authority. It can be applied to the situation where a person who is in fact an agent acts outside their authority; it can also operate to create agency in relation to a person who is not an agent at all. It is a powerful concept, in that it can act retrospectively and affect the legal consequences of actions by third parties that have already taken place, as well as affecting the relationship between principal and agent. For these reasons the concept is subject to various limitations which go some way to ensuring that it does not operate oppressively.[26]

Requirements for ratification

Action must be that of a purported agent

Whether or not the person who performs the act which is to be ratified is an agent or not, they must *purport* to act as such. In other words, the

---

[25] Albeit by a route they had not anticipated.
[26] *Firth v Staines* [1897] 2 QB 70.

agent must expressly or impliedly indicate that they are acting on behalf of someone else. If the third party thinks that the agent is acting independently, then there can be no later ratification. It follows from this that there can never be ratification by an undisclosed principal.

An example of the application of this principle is the case of *Keighley Maxted & Co v Durant*.[27] Roberts, the agent, was authorised by the appellants to buy wheat for their joint account at a certain price. He made a contract with the respondent, Durant, to buy at a higher price. He intended the wheat to be for the joint account, but this fact was not disclosed to Durant. The next day the appellants agreed to take part in the contract, thus purporting to ratify Roberts' unauthorised act. When delivery was subsequently not accepted, Durant sued both Roberts and the appellants. The House of Lords held that where a contract is made by a person intending to contract on behalf of a 'principal', but without the principal's authority, such a contract cannot be ratified so as to render the principal able to sue or liable to be sued on the contract, where the person making the contract did not profess at the time to be acting on behalf of the principal.

This requirement, as Fridman has pointed out,[28] is inconsistent with the acceptance elsewhere in the law of agency that an undisclosed principal can sue or be sued on a contract, even though the third party was, at the time of the contract, totally unaware of the principal's existence.[29] There is perhaps a reluctance to extend that somewhat unusual rule further than is necessary.

It is the appearance of agency rather than the actual intention of the agent that is important. In *Re Tiedemann and Ledermann Frères*[30] the agent purported to act for a named principal in a contract which he in fact intended to be for his own benefit. The other party tried to rescind on the basis of this misrepresentation, but the purported principal ratified the contract and thus prevented the rescission.

This decision makes it difficult to determine the policy that is operating here. While the basic rule that the agent must purport to act for a principal would seem to be designed to protect the third party, in *Re Tiedemann and Ledermann Frères* this was applied in a way which was to the third party's disadvantage. It is unlikely that any injustice would be done by amending the rule so that the agent must not only purport to act for a principal, but must be doing so in fact, before ratification is possible.

---

[27] [1901] AC 240.

[28] *Op cit*, p 75; see also Bowstead, p 58.

[29] See also, Rochvarg (1989) 34 Mc Gill LJ 286.

[30] [1899] 2 QB 66.

The principal must have been in existence at the time of the contract

A principal who did not exist at the time the agent made the contract, purporting to act on behalf of the principal, cannot ratify. This rule is mainly concerned with contracts made on behalf of companies prior to their incorporation, as is shown by the leading authority of *Kelner v Baxter*.[31] The plaintiff was a wine merchant who agreed to supply wine to a hotel, which was to be run by a company of which the plaintiff was to be the manager. A contract to buy wine was purported to be made 'on behalf of the company', which was subsequently incorporated. It was held that the directors who had made the contract were personally liable to the plaintiff for the purchase of the wine. The company could not ratify the contract, since it did not exist at the relevant time. As Willes J commented:

> Putting in the words "on behalf of the Gravesend Royal Alexandra Hotel Company" would operate no more than if a person should contract for a quantity of corn "on behalf of my horses".[32]

Personal liability on pre-incorporation contracts is now governed by statute (ie s 36C of the Companies Act 1985), but this has not affected the common law principle prohibiting ratification, which still prevents a company taking over a contract once it has been incorporated. It has to remain as one between the third party and the promoters in their personal capacity.

The principal must have capacity at the time of the agent's action

In *Firth v Staines*,[33] Wright J stated that for ratification to be valid, 'at the time the act was done the agent must have a competent principal'. Thus, as well as being in existence, the principal must have capacity at the time when the agent purports to act on their behalf to perform the acts done by the agent. However, this rule is of limited practical significance in the modern law.

At one time the rule was important as regard *ultra vires* contracts made on behalf of companies. It meant that neither the Board of Directors, nor the shareholders themselves, could ratify such contracts.[34] This situation is now governed, however, by s 35 of the Companies Act 1985, which effectively removes the *ultra vires* rule (by s 35(1)), and in any case allows for ratification by means of a special resolution (s 35(3)).

---

[31] (1866) LR 2 CP 174.

[32] *Ibid*, at p 185.

[33] [1901] AC 240.

[34] *Rolled Steel Products (Holdings) Ltd v British Steel Corporation* [1982] 3 All ER 1057.

A second situation where the requirement of capacity at the time of the act might be relevant is in relation to minors' contracts. Can a minor, on attaining majority, adopt by ratification an unauthorised contract made on their behalf while still a minor? If the contract was one which is enforceable by a minor, such as a contract for necessary goods or services[35] then the answer must be yes. But what about an unauthorised contract which would have been unenforceable if made by the minor in person? The amendments to the law made by the Minors' Contracts Act 1987 specifically remove the previous statutory prohibition on an adult ratifying, and giving validity to, a contract which they have tried to make while incompetent to do so, because a minor.[36] Bowstead[37] treats the prohibition as applying to ratification of a contract made on behalf of the minor, as well as one made personally. It is not clear, however, that the repeal of the prohibition has changed the position as regards the actions of an agent. It might well be argued that this limitation on ratification is a common law rule, which should be regarded as having been revived following the repeal of the specific statutory position. Thus the minor would not be able to ratify, for example, an unauthorised contract for non-necessary goods made by an agent. The attitude of the courts, if they have to decide the issue, is likely to depend on whether they feel that the general policy of the reforms in the 1987 Act should be taken to have been intended to encompass this particular situation.[38]

The situation as regard contracts made on behalf of the mentally incompetent is also a little unclear. Bowstead asserts that contracts which would be *void* if made by the incompetent individual in person cannot be ratified, whereas those which are *voidable* can.[39] The only authority cited for this is the Australian case of *City Bank of Sydney v McLaughlin*.[40]

There is more certainty in relation to contracts made on behalf of enemy aliens. In *Boston Deep Sea Fishing and Ice Co v Farnham*[41] it was held that a French company could not ratify the acts of a purported agent, since those acts took place in 1940, at which time the French company was classed as an enemy alien, following the occupation of France during the Second World War. The rule that there must have been capacity at the time of the agent's action is thus applied strictly here.

---

35 For a full discussion of contracts which are enforceable by minors, see, eg Treitel *op cit*, Ch 13; Cheshire, Fifoot & Furmston, *op cit*, Ch 13; Stone, *op cit*, Ch 5.

36 Infants Relief Act 1874, s 2.

37 *Op cit*, p 60.

38 See the comments of Markesinis and Munday, *op cit*, p 73.

39 *Op cit*, p 61.

40 (1909) CLR 615.

41 [1957] 3 All ER 204.

The principal must have capacity when the purported ratification takes place

This rule again derives from Wright J in *Firth v Staines*:[42] 'At the time of ratification the principal must be legally capable of doing the act himself.' A minor cannot ratify an unenforceable contract before attaining their majority,[43] nor can a mentally incompetent person do so while still incompetent, or an enemy alien while still an alien. These restrictions are fairly obvious. But note that the rule also means that a person who has *become* an enemy alien or mentally incompetent since the agent's actions, will be unable to ratify, even if the person did not have that status at the time the agent acted.

It seems that lack of 'capacity' under this rule is not limited to legal incompetencies of the kind discussed in the previous section. It can also operate where the principal would have not, as a matter of fact, been able to take the action at the time of ratification. In *Grover & Grover v Matthews*[44] the principal attempted to ratify a contract of fire insurance after a fire had destroyed the property concerned. It was held that the contract could not be ratified, because at the time of the purported ratification the principal would not have been able to make the contract himself.[45] Similarly in *Bird v Brown*[46] ratification of the exercise of a right of stoppage in transit[47] by the agent of an unpaid seller was held to be ineffective, because by the time of ratification the transit had ended. This restriction on ratification has recently been confirmed by the Court of Appeal in *Presentaciones Musicales SA v Secunda*.[48] The restriction did not apply in the case before it, however, which concerned an attempt to ratify an unauthorised issue of a writ, where at the time of ratification the limitation period had expired. This decision was reached on the basis of a more general rule, derived from *Pontin v Wood*,[49] to the effect that procedural defects in a writ can be cured by later action, even beyond the limitation period. A defective writ is not a nullity, and later ratification is therefore possible. This case also confirms the retrospective nature of ratification, discussed below.

---

[42]   [1897] 2 QB 70, at p 75.

[43]   Whether this can be done afterwards is discussed in the previous section.

[44]   [1910] 2 KB 401.

[45]   Note that this does not apply to contracts of marine insurance: *Williams v North China Insurance Co* (1876) 1 CPD 757; Marine Insurance Act 1906.

[46]   (1850) 4 Exch 786, 154 ER 1433.

[47]   See Sale of Goods Act 1979, ss 44–46.

[48]   [1994] 2 All ER 737.

[49]   [1962] 1 All ER 294.

Actions which can be ratified

Subject to the limitations discussed in the previous sections, any actions which could have been taken by the principal may be ratified. The most common situation in which the doctrine can be applied is in relation to the making of contracts. Unless the contract is void *ab initio* (eg because it is for an illegal purpose),[50] then it can be ratified. There is no reason, however, why ratification cannot be used in such a way as to give rise to tortious liability on the part of the principal. As Bowstead points out,[51] the most frequent examples of this are likely to arise in relation to torts which are linked to contracts, such as trespass to goods, or conversion. Suppose, for example, that an agent, without authorisation, buys goods to which the 'seller' had no title, and the principal innocently ratifies the agent's action. The principal will become liable for conversion of the goods.[52] Once it is accepted that there can be liability on this basis, however, there is no reason for it to be limited to such situations. The liability has the potential to apply more generally to the ratification of acts which turn out to be tortious. There seems no reason why a principal may not ratify the unauthorised provision of a service by an agent, and, if the service subsequently turns out to have been delivered negligently, be liable for that negligence.

Conversely, ratification may have the effect of legitimising an act which would otherwise be tortious. A landlord may ratify the action of an agent who has, without authority, levied distress against a tenant in the landlord's name. The action of the agent at the time it took place would clearly be tortious, but the subsequent ratification makes it lawful.[53]

Method of ratification

There are no particular formalities attaching to ratification, except that the execution of a deed can only be ratified by deed.[54] Otherwise, ratification may be express or implied, and the decision as to whether it has occurred or not is essentially one of fact, rather than law. The question is whether the principal's words or deeds (or, indeed, silence or inactivity)[55] indicate an intention to adopt the agent's actions as the principal's own.

---

50 See eg, *Brook v Hook* (1871) LR 6 Exch 89.

51 *Op cit*, p 54.

52 *Hilberry v Hatton* (1864) 2 H&C 822.

53 *Whitehead v Taylor* (1839) 10 Ad & El 210.

54 *Hunter v Parker* (1840) 7 M&W 322; *Mayor, Aldermen, and Citizens of Oxford v Crow* [1893] 3 Ch 535.

55 Eg *Bank Melli Iran v Barclays Bank Ltd* [1951] 2 TLR 1057, at p 1063.

One limitation which exists, however, is that ratification must take place within a reasonable time. Again, this will generally be a question of fact in each case. In relation to contracts, however, it was held in *Metropolitan Asylums Board Managers v Kingham & Sons*[56] that this means ratification must take place before performance of the contract has begun. In that case, a contract for the supply of eggs was due to start on 30 September, but the supplier had tried to withdraw, at a time when acceptance of his offer required ratification. Ratification took place on 6 October. It was held that this was too late. Bowstead doubts whether this should be treated as a firm rule,[57] and indeed it is not that easy to reconcile with *Bolton Partners v Lambert*, discussed in the next section. It is perhaps better to leave the requirement as being that of ratification 'within a reasonable time', with the additional consideration that ratification should not be allowed to prejudice the third party unfairly. This might be a basis for explaining the decision on the facts of *Metropolitan Asylums Board Managers v Kingham & Sons*, without adopting the more specific statement as to the impossibility of ratifying after the date of commencement which appears in the judgment of Fry LJ.[58]

Effect of ratification

Where ratification takes place, the courts will deem the agent's actions to have been authorised at the time they were performed. In other words, ratification is retrospective, and the legal effect of events which occur after the agent's actions but before ratification may be altered. This is illustrated by the case of *Bolton Partners v Lambert*.[59] Bolton Partners owned a factory, which Lambert offered to buy. The offer was accepted by the managing director, who did not in fact have authority to sell on behalf of the Board. The managing director, while purporting to act as agent for the company, had exceeded his authority. On 13 January there was a disagreement, as a consequence of which Lambert withdrew his offer. On 17 January proceedings for breach of contract were started by Bolton Partners. On 28 January the directors ratified the actions of the managing director. Lambert argued that the ratification came too late, because he had already withdrawn from the contract. The Court of Appeal held, however, that the ratification acted retrospectively. The

---

[56] (1890) 6 TLR 217.

[57] *Op cit*, p 77. Note also the *obiter* comments of Parker J in *Bedford Insurance Co Ltd v Instituto de Resseguros do Brasil* [1984] 3 All ER 766, at p 776, and the discussion in Fridman, *op cit*, at p 91.

[58] (1890) 6 TLR 217, at p 218.

[59] (1889) 41 Ch D 295.

course of events had to be considered, therefore, on the basis that the managing director *did* have authority to make the contract at the time that Lambert's offer was accepted. If that was so, there was a binding agreement from that point, and Lambert's attempt to withdraw was ineffective.

Two points are worth noting in relation to this case. First, the rule about reasonable time for ratification was not applied restrictively in this case. It was more that two weeks after Lambert's attempt to withdraw that the ratification took place. Nevertheless, it was held to be effective. Second, although the case may at first sight appear hard on Lambert, closer consideration shows that he was not unduly prejudiced. As far as he was concerned he had made a valid, binding contract from the start. He must have assumed that his attempt to withdraw would be treated as a breach of contract. It is true that in the absence of the retrospective ratification he would have been able to escape from the bargain, but he could not in the end reasonably complain about being held to it.

Although the decision in *Bolton Partners v Lambert* has been the subject of criticism, the Court of Appeal in *Presentaciones Musicales SA v Secunda*[60] confirmed that it remains good law. It seems, however, that the retrospective nature of ratification will not be allowed to affect the vested rights of a person who was a stranger to the original transaction, though the authorities do not establish the point very clearly. In *Presentaciones Musicales SA v Secunda*,[61] this was regarded as one of the justifications for the decision in *Bird v Brown*[62] (the stoppage in transit case).[63] Bowstead[64] illustrates the point with *Donnelly v Popham*,[65] which was concerned with unauthorised appointments within the Royal Navy, but the ruling to this effect appears to be *obiter*. Fridman[66] relies on *Dibbins v Dibbins*,[67] but this decision seems to turn as much on the fact that a specific time limit had expired by the time of the purported ratification. The clearest ruling comes from another case cited by Bowstead, *Re Gloucester Municipal Election Petition, 1900, Forth v Newth*.[68] Here the issue was whether at a particular date Mr Newth, who had been nominated for the town council, had an interest in a contract with the council (which would have disqualified him). A contract had been

---

60 [1994] 2 All ER 737.
61 [1994] 2 All ER 737.
62 (1850) 4 Exch 786.
63 See above, p 29.
64 *Op cit*, p 81.
65 (1807) 1 Taunt 1.
66 *Op cit*, p 88.
67 [1896] 2 Ch 348.
68 [1901] 1 KB 683.

entered into, but Newth had then asked to be released. This had been agreed by a committee of the council, subject to ratification by the full council. Before ratification occurred, Newth's nomination was put in. The question was therefore whether the subsequent ratification had retrospective effect. The court ruled that it did not, because the nomination and election of Newth was a matter of public concern, going beyond the interests of the parties themselves. Where the rights of others might be affected, the general rule as to the retrospective nature of ratification did not apply.

A further, and more clearly established, limitation on the retrospective nature of ratification is illustrated by *Watson v Davies*.[69] The defendant made an offer to sell a house to members of the board of a charity. The members were acting as agents for the charity but, in fact, had no authority to accept the offer. It was therefore stated to be accepted subject to ratification by the full board of the charity. The defendant then withdrew his offer. It was held that a subsequent attempt to ratify the contract was ineffective. Because the original acceptance had been stated to be subject to ratification, the defendant was entitled to withdraw at any time until that ratification took place. The qualification of the acceptance was the distinguishing factor from *Bolton Partners v Lambert*. It also perhaps suggests that it is the perspective of the third party which is important. If the third party thinks that a binding contract has been created, a revocation which is followed by ratification will be ineffective. If, however, the third party is aware of the lack of authority (eg because of a statement that the acceptance is 'subject to ratification') then such a revocation will be allowed, and will prevent subsequent ratification.

Ratification relates primarily to the particular acts ratified, and does not of itself create any agency, or extension of authority, for the future.[70] It may, however, be a factor which can contribute to ostensible authority, discussed in Chapter 4.[71]

AGENCY BY OPERATION OF LAW

There are two situations in which the common law will impose an agency relationship: agency from cohabitation and agency of necessity. There are also various situations where by statute one person is deemed to be the agent of another (as, for example, in a hire-purchase

---

[69] [1931] 1 Ch 455.
[70] *Irvine v Union Bank of Australia* (1877) 2 App Cas 366.
[71] Below, p 98.

transaction, where the dealer is deemed to be the agent of the finance company for certain purposes).[72] In all these cases the relationship of agency arises irrespective of consent or the intentions of the parties. The common law will be dealt with first, and then the statutory rules.

Agency from cohabitation

Agency from cohabitation has links with the concepts of agency by estoppel,[73] and usual authority,[74] but is nevertheless wider than both, and therefore distinct from them. It arises from a presumption that a person who is in charge of the 'domestic management' of a household will have authority to buy necessary goods for that household on behalf of whoever holds the 'purse strings'. The situation appears generally to have been considered in terms of a wife pledging her husband's credit for goods, but it is clearly not limited to that relationship. Indeed in *Debenham v Mellon*,[75] Lord Selborne suggested that the presumption could apply to anyone to whom the domestic management of a household had been delegated, such as 'a housekeeper, or a steward, or any other kind of superior servant'.[76]

The fact that the parties are married does not automatically give rise to the presumption, though this may be the easiest situation from which it may be established. It is also necessary that the goods are ordered for the 'household'. In *Debenham v Mellon* goods were ordered by a wife, but she and her husband were manager and manageress of a hotel, whose basic living expenses were largely met by their employers. In this case there was no 'domestic household', and therefore no presumption of agency. Nor will the presumption arise unless what is supplied comes into the category of 'necessaries'. These have been defined as things that are 'really necessary and suitable to the style in which the [principal] chooses to live'.[77] The category may thus vary according to the principal's lifestyle. The burden of proof is on the supplier.

Even where the presumption does arise on the facts, it can be rebutted in a variety of ways. Some of these were identified by McCardie J, in *Miss Gray Ltd v Earl Cathcart*.[78] The alleged principal may prove that:

---

[72] Consumer Credit Act 1974, s 56; below, p 38.
[73] Below, p 98.
[74] Below, p 103.
[75] (1880) 6 App Cas 24.
[76] *Ibid*, p 33.
[77] *Philipson v Hayter* (1870) LR 6 CP 38.
[78] (1922) 38 TLR 562.

- an express warning has been issued to tradesmen;
- the agent already has sufficient goods of the type supplied;
- the agent had a sufficient allowance so that there was no need to pledge the principal's credit;
- the principal expressly forbade the agent to pledge the principal's credit. This will apparently be effective even if the supplier was unaware of it.

In this case the 'extravagant' and therefore 'unnecessary' purchase of dresses by Lady Cathcart (some 50 or 60 in a year) led the judge to comment that: 'Simplicity [is] an essential feature of useful and beneficent female citizenship ... Prodigality is a feminine fault. It is not a feminine virtue.' As this quotation perhaps illustrates, many of the cases on this type of agency seem to be very much influenced by the social attitudes of their time. There appears to be no reported case on the issue since the 1950s, and so perhaps it is a concept which, while in theory still part of the law, has in practice fallen into desuetude.

Agency of necessity

The second basis on which the common law may impose a relationship of agency without the consent of those involved is on that of 'necessity'. The principle example of this was the power given to a deserted wife to pledge her husband's credit for necessaries. Changes in the divorce and matrimonial property laws, however, introduced other means of protecting the deserted wife, and this type of agency of necessity was abolished by the Matrimonial Proceedings and Property Act 1970, s 41.

The surviving examples of agency of necessity are generally concerned with the power of the agent to act in a situation of emergency to protect property belonging to the principal. This type of situation may arise where the person who takes this action is: (a) already an agent, but has no specific authority to act as he or she does; or (b) is not, prior to that point, an agent of the principal at all.

It may be argued that only cases falling within (b) truly involve the creation of *agency*; those within (a) are simply concerned with the extent of an agent's authority. This is to some extent true, and there would therefore be an argument for discussing category (a) in Chapters 3 and 4. Nevertheless, this category will be dealt with here. There are two justifications for this. First, the facts of the case will often make it difficult to draw a precise division between (a) and (b). Second, the issue of the implied or ostensible authority of an existing agent, discussed in Chapter 4, and which might *prima facie* appear linked with category (a), can in fact be distinguished. Implied and ostensible authority is in the end dependent on the consent of the parties. If the principal and agent act in the appropriate ways towards each other, or towards the outside world, they have the power to set the limits of this kind of authority. True agency of necessity, however, since it is imposed by law, is not dependent on the wishes of the parties. It arises automatically from the factual situation, and cannot be overridden, for example, by a provision in any contract between principal and agent. For these reasons, both category (a) and category (b) cases will be discussed in this chapter.

Another distinction may be drawn between cases where the agent, having acted, is simply seeking compensation from the principal for work done or expenses, and cases where the agent's actions may be found to have brought the principal into a legal relationship (generally contractual) with a third party. As regards the first group, the modern view is that these are better treated as being dealt with by the law relating to 'restitution', than by agency principles.[79] For this reason, discussion here will focus on the second type of case.

The most frequent examples of this type of agency of necessity relate to the actions of shipmasters. Where a cargo is in danger of perishing, for example, the master may be found to have the power to sell it.[80] If the situation is one of agency by necessity, this will bring the owner of the cargo and the purchaser into a contractual relationship. Similarly, if the ship itself is in urgent need of repairs, the master may be forced to mortgage, or even sell, the ship to raise money to carry out the work.[81] Here the contract will be made between the third party and the owner of the ship.

The requirements for this type of agency to be found to exist are:

(a) The existence of a genuine emergency – ie a true 'necessity' for action. The fact that a person acts to avoid inconvenience is insufficient.[82] On the other hand, it is not essential that no other course of action was possible. In *Australian Steam Navigation Co v Morse*[83] the emphasis was put by Sir Montague Smith on the existence of a 'duty' on the agent to take some action to protect the principal's interests. In that context, it was sufficient that what the agent did was in 'the judgment of a wise and prudent man ... apparently the best for the interests of the person for

---

79 See *China Pacific SA v Food Corporation of India, The Winson* [1981] 3 All ER 688, and in particular the comments of Lord Diplock at p 693. See also Bowstead, pp 87–9; Fridman, pp 128–9; Markesinis and Munday, pp 61–62.

80 Eg *The Gratitudine* (1801) 3 CH Rob 240; *Australasian SN Co v Morse* (1872) LR 4 PC 222.

81 Eg *The Australia* (1859) 13 Moo PCC 132; *Gunn v Roberts* (1874) LR 9 CP 331

82 *Sachs v Miklos* [1948] 2 KB 23.

83 (1872) LR 4 PC 222.

whom he acts'.[84] The idea of a 'duty' to act may not be easy to define, but the emphasis on what may be categorised as 'reasonable' behaviour is echoed by the comments of Lindley LJ in *James Phelps & Co v Hill*,[85] where he indicates that necessity means what is 'reasonably necessary' in the light of all the surrounding circumstances.

(b) The impossibility of communication with the principal. The Court of Appeal, in *The Choko Star*,[86] has recently confirmed the importance of this. Given the prevalence of radio communication, and satellite based international telecommunication, this requirement is likely to limit the scope for agency of necessity to arise. The test is whether communication is 'reasonably practicable'. In most circumstances it will be practicable for the agent to get authorisation from the principal before acting. Whether this was so or not, is simply a question of fact.

(c) The agent must have acted *bona fide* in the interests of the principal.[87] The main benefit of the agent's actions must be to the principal, or at least the achievement of such a benefit must be the dominant motive.[88] This formulation indicates that it is not fatal to a claim of agency by necessity, that the agent takes the action for mixed motives, or receives some benefit from it.

Provided that the above requirements are met there seems no reason why agency of necessity should not apply outside the area of shipping contracts. Despite the fact that McCardie J's support for a broadly based doctrine (in *Prager v Blatspiel Stamp & Heacock Ltd*)[89] was firmly rejected by Scrutton LJ in *Jebara v Ottoman Bank*,[90] there are authorities in which it has been assumed that the approach taken in the shipping cases can be applied at least to analogous circumstances arising on land. In *Sachs v Miklos*,[91] for example, a gratuitous bailee sold furniture belonging to the plaintiff in a situation which it was argued amounted to necessity. The court did not accept that necessity was involved, on the facts, but appeared to assume that if it had been such a situation then the doctrine

---

84   *Ibid*, at p 230.
85   [1891] 1 QB 605, at p 610.
86   [1990] 1 Lloyd's Rep 516.
87   *Prager v Blatspiel, Stamp & Heacock Ltd* [1924] 1 KB 566.
88   *China Pacific SA v Food Corpn of India, The Winson* [1982] AC 939.
89   [1924] 1 KB 566.
90   [1927] 2 KB 254.
91   [1948] 1 All ER 67.

of agency of necessity could have applied.[92] More recently, the statement of the principles involved by Lord Simon in *China Pacific SA v Food Corporation of India. The Winson*[93] was in general terms, and not limited to marine cases. He noted that agency of necessity could arise: 'where A is in possession of goods the property of B, and an emergency arises which places those goods in imminent jeopardy'.[94]

Assuming that A cannot obtain instructions from B then A can act in such a way as to bind B to a contract for the sale of the goods, or otherwise make B liable for A's actions as if they were a properly appointed agent.

The conclusion must be that agency of necessity can apply in a range of situations where the principal's goods are threatened. It will, however, be most likely to arise in cases involving shipping contracts. Even here, because of the requirement that the prospective agent makes all reasonable effort to communicate with the prospective principal, the ease of communications in the modern commercial world means that the doctrine will need to be brought into play fairly infrequently.

Agency imposed by statute

The final example of agency by operation of law is where the relationship is imposed by statute. There are no particular principles uniting the situations which have been dealt with in this way, and so it is simply a question of looking at examples.

(a) Insolvency Act 1986. Under s 44(1)(a) of the Insolvency Act 1986, where an administrative receiver has been appointed in relation to a company, they are deemed to be the company's agent, unless and until the company goes into liquidation.

(b) Consumer credit transactions. In *Branwhite v Worcester Works Finance*[95] the court had to consider the place of agency within a hire-purchase contract. As is typical in such arrangements, the hire-purchase agreement was arranged by a dealer, with the eventual contract being made between the purchaser and a finance company. The issue was whether the finance company was responsible for false statements made by the dealer prior to the contract. The House of Lords said that it was not, because the

---

92 *Cf* also *Munro v Wilmott* [1948] 2 All ER 983. Some other cases are cited by Fridman, at pp 124–5 as possible examples, but can be explained as cases of implied authority. *Cf* Bowstead, p 86.

93 [1981] 3 All ER 688.

94 *Ibid*, at p 697.

95 [1968] 3 All ER 104.

dealer was not acting as its agent. On the contrary, the dealer was the agent of the purchaser, with the finance company therefore playing the role of 'third party'. There was some unhappiness with this decision, and the opportunity was taken in the Consumer Credit Act 1974 to reverse its effect to some extent. Section 56(2) of the Act provides that: 'Negotiations with the debtor in a case falling within subsection 1(1)(b) or subsection 1(1)(c) shall be deemed to be conducted by the negotiator in the capacity of agent of the creditor as well as in his actual capacity.'

The circumstances referred to in s 56(1) are where the 'negotiator', or 'dealer', makes statements in antecedent negotiations which lead to the hire-purchase agreement or other contract for the supply of goods on credit.

CHAPTER 3

PRINCIPAL AND AGENT

INTRODUCTION

This chapter is concerned with the rights and obligations that arise out of the agency relationship itself. What powers does the agent have, and what duties are imposed on the agent? When is the principal obliged to pay commission? What other duties does the principal have? We start by looking at the relationship from the perspective of the agent, and then consider the position of the principal.

THE POWERS AND OBLIGATIONS OF THE AGENT

Authority

The first issue to consider is that of the agent's authority to act on behalf of the principal. This is at the centre of the concept of agency. The issue of 'authority' will be considered further in Chapter 4, in connection with the relationship between principal and third party. There the focus will be on the extent to which a third party is entitled to hold the principal liable to contracts negotiated by the agent, or in other ways to make the principal responsible for the agent's actions.[1] In this chapter, however, we are concerned simply with the relationship between principal and agent. If the agent exceeds authority, the principal may still be liable to the third party, but may have an action against the agent. The agent may be in breach of contract, and liable to pay damages, if that is the way in which the relationship was created. In any case, the principal may well be entitled to terminate the relationship, and refuse to pay commission.[2]

It is thus important to identify the scope of the agent's authority. The authority may be express or implied.

---

[1] Eg in tort. See p 111.

[2] But see below, p 85, as to the agent's right to commission and the right to compensation on termination resulting from EC law p 163.

Express authority

Authority may be given by deed (particularly in relation to powers of attorney), by some other contractual or non-contractual document, or orally. In respect of powers of attorney the tendency has been to interpret these strictly, and not to give the agent any wider power than is clearly contained in the grant. Thus, an agent given the power to buy goods for a business, and deal with bills of exchange or promissory notes in this connection, has no power to borrow money.[3] Similarly, in *Reckitt v Barnett*[4] a letter to a bank indicating that an agent with power of attorney had authority to draw cheques without restriction did not give authority for the agent to draw cheques in relation to the agent's own debts.

Bowstead suggests that this approach may result from the recognition that in the commercial sphere 'powers of attorney tend to be drawn by lawyers and use technical wording which may be assumed to have been carefully chosen'.[5] And in relation to non-commercial powers of attorney, where the principal may be ill, or otherwise incapacitated, it may be the case that a policy of protecting the principal is justifiable.

It is clear, however, that the same approach does not apply to authority given other than by deed. Here the courts tend to interpret the authority much more flexibly, whether it is given orally,[6] or in writing.[7] If, as in *Ireland v Livingston*,[8] the principal's instructions are ambiguous, the agent who follows, in good faith, one of the possible constructions, will be held to be acting within the express authority. In *Ireland v Livingston* the basic instruction was to buy 500 tons of sugar in Mauritius, and ship it to Britain. The principal also indicated, however, that there might be a variation in the amount, by '50 tons more or less', if this enabled the agent to secure a suitable vessel. The agent shipped 400 tons in a vessel carrying other cargo, and this was held to be within his authority. As Lord Chelmsford put it:[9]

> If a principal gives an order to an agent in such uncertain terms as to be susceptible of two different meanings, and the agent *bona fide* adopts one of them and acts upon it, it is not competent to the principal to repudiate the act as unauthorised because he meant it to be read in the other sense of which it is equally capable.

---

3   *Jacobs v Morris* [1902] 1 Ch 816.
4   [1929] AC 1.
5   *Op cit*, pp 99–100.
6   As in *Pole v Leask* (1863) 33 LJ Ch 155.
7   Eg *Boden v French* (1851) 10 CB 886.
8   (1872) LR 5 HL 395.
9   At p 416.

In interpreting what the principal meant, the court will look at all the surrounding circumstances.The fact that the particular transaction which has apparently been authorised is not possible in a particular market may mean that the agent can act with authority in making a contract which is very close to that specified. In *Johnston v Kershaw*,[10] for example, the agent was instructed to purchase 100 bales of cotton at Pernambuco, in Brazil. It was apparently not normally possible to purchase 100 bales at Pernambuco. The purchase of 94 bales was held to be authorised.

In this case, the surrounding circumstances acted to expand the literal meaning of the authority. The process can, however, also operate to *restrict* an apparently clear authority. In *Wiltshire v Sims*[11] an instruction to a stockbroker to sell stock or shares was held not to include an authority to sell on credit, because stockbrokers do not usually have such authority.

The delineation of an agent's express authority thus involves interpreting the words and actions of the principal in the light of the surrounding circumstances. The approach does not depend solely on discerning the principal's intentions; rather, the test is an objective one. The question to be asked is 'How would a reasonable agent interpret these instructions in the light of all the circumstances?'. The answer to that question will indicate the scope of the agent's express authority.

Implied authority

Implied authority is of two types. First, the agent will be regarded (in the absence of any express instruction to the contrary) as having the authority to do anything which is necessarily incidental to the express authority. Second (and again in the absence of any contrary instruction) the agent will be implied to have such authority as is usual, or customary, for an agent carrying out the business in question or operating in a particular place or market.

In considering this topic, it must be remembered that, although issues of implied authority will commonly arise where a third party is trying to enforce a contract against a principal, that is not the focus in this chapter. That aspect of implied authority is discussed in Chapter 4.[12] Here we are concerned solely with the relationship between principal and agent. The main difference is that, as between these two parties, the authority can always be limited by an express instruction from the principal to the agent. As will be seen in Chapter 4, however, this may

---

[10] (1867) LR 2 Ex 82.

[11] (1808) 1 Camp 258

[12] Below, p 103.

not in itself be sufficient to prevent a third party from relying on the implied authority. The case of *Waugh v Clifford*[13] provides a good example of this distinction.

The dispute was between the builders of some houses and the purchasers who alleged negligence on the part of the builders. The action was compromised by the builders' solicitors on the basis of the houses being bought back at a price to be fixed by an independent valuer. In fact the builders had given express instructions not to compromise on the basis of independent valuation. The Court of Appeal, with Brightman J giving the main judgment, pointed out that there might be a difference between a solicitor's implied authority *vis-à-vis* his client, and his ostensible authority *vis-à-vis* a third party. For example, if in a defamation action, the defendant's solicitor offered £100,000 in settlement:

> It would in my view be officious on the part of the plaintiff's solicitor to demand to be satisfied as to the authority of the defendant's solicitor to make the offer. It is perfectly clear that the defendant's solicitor has *ostensible* authority to compromise the action on behalf of his client, notwithstanding the large sum involved ... But it does not follow that the defendant's solicitor would have *implied* authority to agree to damages on that scale without the agreement of his client. In the light of the solicitor's knowledge of his client's cash position it might be quite unreasonable and indeed grossly negligent for the solicitor to commit his client to such a burden without first inquiring if it were acceptable ... It follows in my view that a solicitor (or counsel) may in a particular case have ostensible authority *vis-à-vis* the opposing litigant where he has no implied authority *vis-à-vis* his client.[14]

This case makes it clear that the fact that the implied authority existing between principal and agent may often be co-terminous with the agent's ostensible authority should not lead one into the error of thinking that they are one and the same.

The two types of implied authority will now be considered in turn.

Authority necessarily incidental to express authority

If an agent is employed to buy goods, and is given a range of prices at which they may be purchased, it is a necessary incident of such authority that the agent can negotiate on price with third parties. Similarly an agent who is authorised to sell a piece of land must also be

---

13 [1982] Ch 374.
14 *Ibid*, at p 387.

authorised to carry out the formalities (signing documents, etc) which will make such a transaction effective.[15] In other words, the agent must be presumed to have authority to take all steps necessary towards the achievement of the overall objective (or objectives) of the agency.

There are two limitations on this which must be noted. First, the implied authority will be limited to what *necessarily* follows from the principal's instructions: it does not cover what might simply be reasonable. Thus in *Hamer v Sharp*[16] an agent had been engaged to 'find a purchaser'. This was held not to include the authority to conclude a sale of the property. Similarly, the view was expressed in *Benmag Ltd v Barda*[17] that an agent who was employed to sell goods 'by description' would have no implied authority to warrant their quality.[18]

Second, the authority may be limited by the agent's own knowledge. As in the example quoted from *Waugh v Clifford*, above, the agent may be aware of circumstances which mean that an authority which would normally be implied (eg to compromise an action on certain terms) would not in fact be acceptable to the principal. As with express authority given other than by deed, the interpretation of implied authority of this type of implied authority must be limited by what a reasonable agent would take to be authorised.

Authority arising from the agent's type of work or place of business

Lord Denning, in *Hely-Hutchinson v Brayhead*,[19] stated that when the board of directors of a company appoint one of their number to be managing director, they 'thereby impliedly authorise him to do all such things as fall within the usual scope of that office'. What 'things' do fall within the 'usual' scope of the post will be a question of fact, to be determined in each case. The quotation confirms, however, that an agent may have a certain area of implied authority simply through being employed in a particular position. Unless the principal takes steps to impose an express limitation, the agent will be entitled to do any acts within the scope of such implied authority. This type of authority has often been classified by commentators, though not generally by the courts, as 'usual authority'.[20] It refers to the authority 'usually' attaching

---

15 *Rosenbaum v Belson* [1900] 2 Ch 267.

16 (1874) LR 19 Eq 108.

17 [1955] 2 Lloyd's Rep 354.

18 Further examples of this kind of limitation on implied authority may be found in Bowstead, p 105.

19 [1967] 3 All ER 98.

20 See Bowstead, p 95; Fridman, p 60.

to a particular position. Bowstead[21] draws a distinction between those holding a particular post within an organisation, such as a director of a company, a matron of a hospital,[22] or a local authority engineer,[23] and those who are acting as agents in the course of an independent trade, profession, or business, such as solicitors, bailiffs, auctioneers or architects. It is submitted, however, that the distinction does not relate to any difference in principle between the different types of agent in terms of identifying implied authority. In each case it is simply a question of fact as to what would be the usual authority to expect an agent to have in that situation. A manager of an estate may, for example, usually have authority to give and receive notices to quit.[24] Similarly, a solicitor will usually have implied actual authority to receive information relating to a conveyancing transaction,[25] or to settle litigation.[26] The manager comes within Bowstead's first category, and the solicitor the second, but there is no real difference in the process of identifying usual authority in each case, and the principles applying to this area operate in the same way in both situations. Once it has been established as a matter of fact that the particular actions taken fall within the agent's usual authority, then, in the absence of any express limitation by the principal, the manager or solicitor will be impliedly authorised to act in this way.

Customary authority

Here the implication of authority arises, not from the nature of the agent's work, but the place or market in which it is carried out. Particular places, and particular markets, have their own traditions, and, in the absence of express contradiction, an agent's authority will be interpreted in accordance with these. It is not necessary that the principal is aware of the custom,[27] it will still operate to define the agent's authority. The establishment of the custom will, as with usual authority, be largely a question of fact, but if, as a matter of law the custom is held to be unreasonable,[28] or unlawful,[29] it will not normally be effective. The only clear exception to this is where the principal is aware of an unreasonable custom, and may be said therefore to have

---

21 *Op cit* at pp 108–114.

22 Eg *Real and Personal Advance Co v Phalempin* (1893) 9 TLR 569.

23 Eg *Ashford Shire Council v Dependable Motors Pty Ltd* [1961] AC 336.

24 *Papillon v Brunton* (1860) 5 H&N 518.

25 *Strover v Harrington* [1988] 1 All ER 769.

26 *Waugh v Clifford* [1982] Ch 374.

27 *Bayliffe v Butterworth* (1847) 17 LJ Ex 78; see below, p 80.

28 Eg *Robinson v Mollett* (1874) LR 7 HL 802.

29 *Bailey v Rawlins* (1829) 7 LJ (os) KB 208.

agreed to its operation.[30] There are also some old cases which suggest that in certain circumstances a principal can also waive the *illegality* of a custom,[31] but this seems wrong in principle, and the better view must be that illegality will always prevent a custom taking effect.

An example of a custom which was held to be effective is *Cropper v Crook*.[32] The agent was a broker buying wool in the Liverpool market. It was a custom of that market that the broker may buy either in their own name, or that of the principal, without any need to notify the principal of this. It was held that there was nothing unreasonable in this custom, and the broker was therefore acting with implied authority in making in his own name a contract, which was in fact made on behalf of the principal.[33]

In *Sweeting v Pearce*,[34] on the other hand, a custom operating in the Lloyd's insurance market was held to be unreasonable. This was that a broker who was authorised to receive money from underwriters on behalf of a principal, could settle the account by means of a 'set-off', ie a debt owed by the broker personally to the underwriters. It was held that the broker would be acting without authority in agreeing the settlement on this basis, unless the principal was aware of the custom.[35]

The duty to obey instructions

One of the central duties of an agent is to carry out the principal's instructions properly. Where the agency is created by contract, this will be a contractual obligation. As far as commercial agents, within the meaning of the Commercial Agents (Council Directive) Regulations 1993[36] are concerned, this duty is imposed by reg 3(2). The commercial agent must 'make proper efforts to negotiate and, where appropriate, conclude the transactions he is instructed to take care of,' and must 'comply with reasonable instructions given by his principal'.

A gratuitous agent will not be liable simply for failure to perform,[37] but may, like a contractual agent, be liable for exceeding authority, or

---

30 *Hamilton v Young* (1881) 7 LR Ir 289.
31 See the cases on the Banking Companies (Shares) Act 1867 (now repealed), noted in Bowstead, at p 116.
32 (1868) LR 3 CP 194.
33 A further example is *Scott and Horton v Godfrey* [1901] 2 KB 726, discussed in Chapter 4, p 105.
34 (1859) 7 CB (NS) 449.
35 Cf *Pearson v Scott* (1878).
36 The background to these regulations and the definition of 'commercial agent' contained in the, are discussed in Chapter 1, at p 13.
37 *Coggs v Bernard* (1703) 2 Ld Raym. 909; *Balfe v West* (1853) 13 CB 466.

failing to exercise proper care and skill. The question of the limits of the agent's authority has been discussed in the previous section, so it does not require further consideration here. In this section we concentrate on the contractual agent's duty to carry out instructions, and the general duty to take reasonable care in performance.

Duty to perform

This is a duty that only applies to agents who are operating under contract. The contract itself will, expressly or impliedly, impose obligations on the agent, and define the limits of the agent's authority. If the agent fails to do what is expected, the agent will be liable to the principal. An example is the case of *Fraser v Furman*.[38] The agents were insurance brokers who failed to effect an insurance policy for certain employers (the principal). As a result the principal had to pay compensation to an injured employee and claimed the cost of this from the brokers. The brokers attempted to argue that even if the policy had been taken out, the employers would have been in breach of a condition in it which required that 'the insured shall take reasonable precautions to prevent accident and disease', and that the insurers would have therefore refused to pay. On the facts, the Court of Appeal refused to accept that the insurers would have acted in this way, and so held the brokers liable. The principle behind the brokers' argument, however, was not rejected, and it must presumably be the case that if the causal link between the agent's failure to act, and the principal's loss, cannot be established, there will be no liability. The breach of the duty to perform will not in itself entitle the principal to substantial damages.

A similar failure to perform occurred in *Turpin v Bilton*,[39] where the agent did not act sufficiently quickly to insure a ship, with the result that when it was lost the owner was uninsured. The agent was liable for the failure to act. There are *dicta* in the case, however, from Tindal CJ,[40] which suggest that the agent would not have been liable if he had tried to insure, but had failed to find anyone willing to underwrite the risk. It must be true that if the obligations of the agency contract are impossible to perform, then it will be frustrated, and obligations under it will be discharged. This point must be distinguished, however, from the question of whether the agent's obligation is to *achieve* a particular result (eg the agreement of an insurance contract), or to *take reasonable steps towards* achieving that result. This will depend on the proper

---

[38] (1967) 3 All ER 57.
[39] (1843) 5 Man & G 455.
[40] *Ibid*, at p 470.

interpretation of the principal's instructions, whether these are contained in the contract creating the agency, or given subsequently.

The agent cannot justify a failure to act on the basis that the instructions involve acting in a way which the agent regards as inadvisable,[41] or foolish.[42] Equally, however, the agent will not be liable for acting in a way which causes the principal a loss, provided that the action is in accordance with the principal's instructions. Thus in *Overend, Gurney & Co v Gibb*,[43] a director who went ahead, in accordance with instructions, with the purchase of a partnership which was in very great financial difficulties, was not liable to the company (his principal) for having done so.[44]

On the other hand the agent will not be in breach for failing to follow instructions which would involve acting illegally. There does not appear to be any specific authority on this point, but it will come under the general restriction in the law of contract on illegal agreements.[45] Equally, an omission by the agent to make a contract which is regarded as being void and unenforceable will not give the principal any right of action against the agent. The authority for this is *Cohen v Kittell*.[46] The agent was employed to place bets. Such transactions were void and unenforceable under the Gaming Act 1845. The agent failed to place the bets, and the principal sued for the money he would have won. Huddleston B treated this as being the equivalent of employing the agent to do an illegal act: 'The breach of such a contract by the agent can give no right of action to the principal'.[47] If the bet is placed, and is successful, however, the agent who receives the winnings is obliged to hand them over to the principal: *Bridger v Savage*.[48]

Duty to act with due care and skill

This duty applies to both contractual and gratuitous agents, though, as will be seen, it has been suggested that the standard of care may be different. For that reason, the duties will be considered separately.

---

41 *Fray v Voules* (1859) 1 E&E 839 (compromise of legal action, contrary to instructions); see also *Swinfen v Lord Chelmsford* (1860) 5 H&N 890.

42 *RH Deacon & Co Ltd v Varga* (1927) 30 DLR (3d) 653.

43 (1872) LR 5 HL 480.

44 NB, however, the duty to act with proper care and skill, noted below.

45 See eg Treitel, *The Law of Contract*, 9th edn, Ch 11; Stone, *Contract Law*, Ch 10.

46 (1889) 22 QBD 680.

47 *Ibid*, at p 683.

48 (1885) 15 QBD 363.

Contractual agents

The standard expected of the contractual agent is to take reasonable care in performing the duties imposed by the contract. At one time it was thought that this duty was purely contractual.[49] The expansion of the tort of negligence in the 1970s, however, led to the view that an agent could also be liable on this basis for a failure to take reasonable care in acting for the principal. The possibility of such simultaneous liability was confirmed by the Court of Appeal in *Esso Petroleum Co Ltd v Mardon*.[50] Despite the fact that, more recently, caution has been expressed about always imposing tortious liability on contracting parties, particularly where the contract has been carefully negotiated,[51] and the fact that there has been a retreat from a broadly based tort of negligence to one based incrementally on the recognition of particular categories of duties of care,[52] the decision of the House of Lords in *Henderson v Merrett Syndicates Ltd*[53] indicates that such twin liability can still exist. Since, however, the standard of care in both contract and tort will be to take such care as is reasonable in the circumstances, the existence of the alternative bases for action will only be of significance where issues of limitation arise. This is because in contract time starts to run as soon as the contract has been broken, whereas in the tort of negligence it does not do so until some damage has resulted from the tortious act. Thus the tortious action may survive after the contractual one has become time-barred.

As has been indicated, the expectation of 'due care and skill' means that the agent must act with such care as is reasonable in all the circumstances. What it is reasonable to expect will depend on the type of agent concerned. The test was expressed in *Beal v South Devon Ry Co*[54] in the following terms:

> In the case of a carrier or other agent holding himself out for the careful and skillful performance of a particular duty, gross negligence includes the want of that reasonable care, skill and expedition, which may properly be expected from persons so holding themselves out and their servants.

---

[49] See, eg *Bagot v Stevens, Scanlon & Co Ltd* [1966] 1 QB 197.

[50] [1976] QB 801. See also cases such as *Midland Bank Trust Co Ltd v Hett, Stubbs & Kemp* [1979] Ch 384.

[51] *Tai Hing Cotton Mill Ltd v Liu Chong Hing Bank Ltd* [1986] AC 80.

[52] See *Murphy v Brentwood* [1991] AC 398, where the House of Lords rejected the broader approach taken in *Anns v Merton London BC* [1978] AC 728.

[53] [1994] 3 All ER 506.

[54] (1864) 3 H&C 337, at 341.

The standard is therefore an objective one. A solicitor, for example, must act with the care that the public has been led to expect of a person exercising this profession.[55] Thus in relation to the normal duties of a solicitor, such as carrying out conveyancing, or conducting litigation, a general standard will apply. Particular circumstances, however, may affect the situation, and extend the scope of the duty. While a solicitor might not normally be expected to advise on investments in stocks and shares, and therefore the standard of care would be relatively low in relation to such advice, if they are held out as having expertise in such matters, then the standard may increase to that reasonably to be expected of a stockbroker. Likewise, an insurance broker who decides to give advice on insurance law, must take reasonable care to ensure it is correct.[56]

The test is therefore in part based on a question of fact. What is reasonably to be expected of a person exercising the trade or profession of this agent? If the agent is employed for general commercial activities, and not as a result of any actual or professed competence, the test will simply be what the court considers to be reasonable behaviour by this particular agent in these circumstances. In either case, however, there must be added any particular circumstances that affect the case under consideration, and any terms in the contract between principal and agent that may relate to liability. Any attempts to *exclude* or *limit* the agent's liability will be subject to the provisions of the Unfair Contract Terms Act 1977, particularly as they relate to negligence.[57] Such exclusions or limitations will in general be subject to the test of reasonableness as set out in s 11 of that Act.

Gratuitous agents

The liability of a gratuitous agent cannot, by definition, arise in contract, and therefore must be tortious. The liability of the gratuitous agent as regards failure to exercise the appropriate care and skill is stated in the current edition of Bowstead,[58] Article 44(3),[59] in the following terms (emphasis added):

> The degree of care and skill owed by a gratuitous agent to his principal is *such skill and care as persons ordinarily exercise in their own affairs* or, where the agent has expressly or impliedly held himself

---

[55] *Simmons v Pennington* [1955] 1 WLR 183.

[56] *Sarginson Bros v Keith Moulton & Co* (1942) LL L Rep 104.

[57] Ie s 2.

[58] Ie the 15th, published in 1985.

[59] *Op cit*, p 152.

out to his principal as possessing skill adequate to the performance of a particular undertaking, such skill and care as would normally be shown by one possessing that skill.

This is derived from statements by Holt CJ in *Coggs v Bernard*,[60] but its accuracy in the modern law is doubted by the current editor of Bowstead in his commentary,[61] and the emphasised part of the article, suggesting that a gratuitous agent need only act as they would have done if acting on their own behalf, must certainly be reconsidered in the light of the decision in *Chaudhry v Prabhakar*.[62] The plaintiff wanted to buy a second-hand car, but was not particularly knowledgeable in such matters. She therefore asked a friend to try to find a suitable car for her. This friend in fact worked in a grocer's shop, but, as the plaintiff knew, had some apparently successful experience of buying and selling cars. She stipulated that the car must not have been involved in an accident. The friend agreed to try to find a car. No payment for this was to be involved. May LJ, in the Court of Appeal, was very dubious as to whether this arrangement should properly be regarded as involving any legal duty on the part of the friend.[63] It was accepted by both sides, however, that the friend was acting as a gratuitous agent, and the rights and liabilities had therefore to be determined on this basis. The friend had found a car, which he advised the plaintiff to buy. It was in the possession of a panel-beater, and the friend was aware that the bonnet had been repaired or replaced. He persuaded the plaintiff to buy the car, without having it examined by a mechanic. It later transpired that the car had been involved in a serious accident, had been very badly repaired, and was unroadworthy. The plaintiff sued both the person who sold the car, and her friend. The friend's defence was that he was simply a gratuitous agent. As such, it was argued that his only duty was to act as carefully as he would have done on his own behalf. If he was believed in his assertion that he would have bought the car himself, he would be under no liability as regards the plaintiff.

The Court of Appeal refused to accept this interpretation of the obligations of the gratuitous agent. Stuart-Smith LJ, who delivered the main judgment, preferred to regard the standard as an objective one. Thus, in relation to *all* agents, the duty is to take such care as may reasonably be expected of that agent in all the circumstances.[64] Whether

---

[60] (1703) 2 Ld Raym 909.

[61] *Op cit*, pp 154–5.

[62] [1988] 3 All ER 718.

[63] *Ibid*, p 725

[64] Both Stuart-Smith LJ and Socker LJ draw analogies with the situation in relation to gratuitous bailment, and the similar test stated by Ormerod LJ in *Houghlan v RR Low (Luxury Coaches) Ltd* [1962] 2 All ER 159.

or not the agent is paid is simply one of the relevant circumstances that affects the duty. Here, since what was involved was essentially negligent advice, the standard was in effect the same as applied in relation to negligent misstatements under *Hedley Byrne v Heller*.[65] On the facts, the friend had not taken reasonable care. He had not asked the seller whether the car had been involved in an accident, and specifically told the plaintiff that it had not been, despite the fact that he should have been put on notice by the fact that he knew the bonnet had been repaired. He was in breach of his duty as a gratuitous agent, and was liable in damages to the plaintiff.

This Court of Appeal decision must be taken as representing the current law on this issue. In effect, therefore, the standard of care should be stated in the same way for both paid and gratuitous agents. It is to take such care as is reasonable in all the circumstances. The fact that the agent is unpaid is a relevant circumstance, which will reduce the level of care to be regarded as reasonable. The obligations, however, may go beyond acting honestly in the way in which the agent would have done if acting on their own behalf.

It is arguable that in practice this means that there is no difference between the duty imposed on paid and unpaid agent. If the friend in *Chaudry v Prabhakar* had been paid by the plaintiff, would the standard of care have been any higher? It is hard to see that it would have been. Indeed, Stuart-Smith LJ places emphasis on the skill and experience possessed, or professed, by the agent as a very significant circumstance. This will be so whether or not the agent is paid. A contractual agent may have specific obligations under the contract, but otherwise the distinction between the paid and unpaid agent seems to have been blurred, if not destroyed, by this decision.

Duty of non-delegation

The relationship between principal and agent is personal. The agent is not generally entitled, unless having express or implied authority to do so, to delegate to someone else the tasks given to them by the principal. This is sometimes expressed in the Latin maxim *delegatus non potest delegare*, which is of more general application in English law than simply in relation to agency.[66] If an agent delegates without authority, there is no privity between the 'sub-agent' and the principal, and the agent will be in breach of the agency relationship, and remain liable for all obligations arising under it.[67] The actions of the delegate will be a

---

[65] [1963] 2 All ER 575.

[66] It applies also, for example, in administrative law.

[67] *Caitlin v Bell* (1815) 4 Camp 183.

nullity, and will not give a third party effected by them any right of action against the principal or agent, unless ostensible authority can be established.[68]

Authorised delegation

The agent may have express authority to delegate, or the principal may subsequently ratify an unauthorised delegation, as in *Keay v Fenwick*,[69] (where an agent sold a ship through a broker). The obligations which may thus arise between agent and sub-agent are considered below. First, however, it is necessary to consider the situations where a power to delegate may be implied.

The most general type of implication arises where the act which is delegated can be regarded as purely 'ministerial'. This means that the delegate is simply the means by which the agent acts, and is not exercising any discretion in relation to what is done. In *John McCann & Co v Pow*[70] an estate agent acting for a vendor was not entitled to delegate powers to another firm of estate agents, because these powers were not ministerial. In *Allam & Co v Europa Poster Services Ltd*,[71] however, the agent delegated to solicitors the power to give notice of the termination of certain licences. It was held that this was a purely ministerial act. The delegation was impliedly authorised, and the notices of termination were therefore effective.

Delegation may also be authorised by the nature of the agent. If the agent is a company, or other incorporeal legal person, it will be necessary for it to act through human agents, to whom its powers will be delegated. A similar necessity for delegation may arise where the agent is to be engaged to perform actions which are to take place in another country.[72] Furthermore, the custom of a particular trade or profession may allow for delegation by certain types of agent.[73]

The particular circumstances surrounding the case may imply that delegation is allowed. This will be so if, for example, the principal is aware at the time that the agency is created that the agent intends to delegate.[74] More generally, the behaviour of the parties may lead to an implication that delegation was permitted. Such an implication may also derive from the fact that delegation becomes necessary as a result of

---

[68] See Chapter 4, p 98.
[69] (1876) 1 CPD 745.
[70] [1975] 1 All ER 129.
[71] [1968] 1 All ER 826.
[72] *Quebec & Richmond Rly Co v Quinn* (1858) 12 Moo PC 232.
[73] *De Bussche v Alt* (1878) 8 Ch D 286; *Solley v Wood* (1852) 16 Beav 370.
[74] *Quebec & Richmond Rly Co v Quinn* (1858) 12 Moo PC 232.

unforeseen circumstances. These last two categories were recognised by Thesiger J in *De Bussche v Alt*,[75] and clearly make good sense, but there do not seem to be any clear examples of their application in reported cases.

Effect of authorised delegation

Where delegation is authorised, does this produce any rights and liabilities as between the sub-agent and the principal? In general the answer seems to be that it does not, but, as is shown by one of the leading cases in this area, *De Bussche v Alt*,[76] in some circumstances it may. The plaintiff consigned a ship to an agent, Gilman & Co, in China, with instructions for it to be sold at a minimum price of $90,000. With the knowledge and consent of the plaintiffs, Gilman & Co employed the defendants, in Japan, to sell the ship, with the same instructions. The defendants failed to find a buyer and bought it themselves for $90,000. Shortly afterwards, they resold it for $160,000. The plaintiffs sued for the profit on the transaction. It was held that the defendant was liable to account for the profit, in the same way as an agent appointed directly by the principal.[77]

As has been indicated, this result is unusual. More commonly the courts have held that there is no privity between principal and sub-agent. In other words, there are two relationships, principal/agent, and agent/sub-agent. Within each of these rights and duties exist, but no overarching relationship between principal and sub-agent is generally created. Thus, if a sub-agent fails to perform, the principal may hold the agent responsible, though the agent in turn may have a right of action against the sub-agent. The principal cannot, however, sue the sub-agent directly. This was the view taken by Wright J in *Calico Printers' Association Ltd v Barclays Bank*,[78] where the sub-agent failed to insure goods. It follows a similar line taken in earlier cases such as *New Zealand & Australian Land Co v Watson*[79] (sub-agent not liable to account to principal for the proceeds of goods sold), and *Lockwood v Abdy*[80] (solicitor sub-agent not liable to account for management of the principal's affairs, even though he had been in direct communication with the principal). The decision in *De Bussche v Alt* is thus clearly exceptional. The finding of a direct obligation from sub-agent to

---

75 (1878) 8 Ch D 286.
76 *Ibid.*
77 For the duty to account for secret profits, see below, p 61.
78 (1931) 145 LT 51, at 55.
79 (1881) 7 QBD 374.
80 (1845) 14 Sim 437.

principal will, it seems, only occur where it is established 'not only that the principal contemplated that the sub-agent would perform part of the contract, but also that the principal authorised the agent to create privity of contract between the principal and sub-agent, which is a very different matter requiring precise proof'.[81]

At one time it seemed that the tort of negligence might develop in a way that allowed a principal to sue a negligent sub-agent who had caused purely economic loss, even where there was not privity. The high-watermark of this approach was the House of Lords decision in *Junior Books v Veitchi Co Ltd*,[82] where a sub-contractor was held liable to the owner of premises for economic loss caused by negligent work. The appellate courts have, however, subsequently retreated from this position, with a member of the Court of Appeal in one case of doubting the relevance of *Junior Books* to any case outside its own particular facts.[83] The House of Lords has not, however, gone so far as to overrule the decision, but has greatly restricted the scope of recovery in negligence for pure economic loss.[84] In line with this trend, in *Balsamo v Medici*[85] a sub-agent was held not to be liable to the principal in relation to money received in respect of a sale of the principal's property, even though it was arguable that the sub-agent had acted negligently in parting with the money to a fraudulent third party. There was no duty of care owed by the sub-agent to the principal in tort. Since there was no privity between them either, the principal's only available remedies were against the agent, rather than the sub-agent.

This decision must now, however, be looked at in the light of the House of Lords' speeches in *Henderson v Merrett Syndicates Ltd*.[86] The case arose out the collapse in the Lloyd's insurance market, and the substantial losses suffered as a result by 'names' who had invested money in the market. One of the principal issues was whether the agents or sub-agents who managed the insurance business on behalf of the names were potentially liable in the tort of negligence, as well as in contract. The House of Lords had no doubt that this was a situation where *Hedley Byrne v Heller*[87] applied. The agents and sub-agents could be taken to have assumed a responsibility towards the names to perform

---

81   *Calico Printer's Association Ltd v Barclays Bank* (1931) 145 LT 51, at 55, *per* Wright J.

82   [1983] 1 AC 520. See Bowstead, *op cit*, pp 133.

83   Dillon LJ, in *Simaan General Contracting Co v Pilkington Glass Ltd (No 2)* [1988] 1 All ER 791, at 805: 'I find it difficult to see that future citation from *Junior Books* can ever serve any useful purpose'.

84   See eg *D & F Estates Ltd v Church Commissioners for England* [1988] 2 All ER 992; *Murphy v Brentwood DC* [1990] 2 All ER 908.

85   [1984] 2 All ER 304.

86   [1994] 3 All ER 506.

87   [1963] 2 All ER 575.

professional or quasi-professional services, and thus were under a duty of care. They could, therefore, be liable for purely economic losses suffered by the names as a result of the agents' or sub-agents' negligence, independent of any liability in contract. If there was a contractual relationship this could modify the tortious duty, but the mere existence of the contract did not stop it arising.

The case clearly establishes that in certain circumstances a sub-agent can be liable to the principal in tort for pure economic loss. It is not clear, however, what the effect of this is on *Balsamo v Medici*, which, somewhat surprisingly, was not cited in *Henderson v Merrett*. The latter decision does not necessarily mean that *Balsamo v Medici* was wrongly decided. Whether there is a duty of care owed by the sub-agent in any particular case will depend on the circumstances. In *Balsamo v Medici* the sub-agent was concerned simply with commercial activities, rather than providing professional advice, or other services of a similar kind, and it may well be that this is an important distinguishing factor. The sub-agents in *Henderson v Merrett* had held themselves out as having special expertise to advise on the placing of insurance business, and the risks involved in it, and it was that assumption of responsibility which the House of Lords felt indicated that they were under a duty of care towards their principals, the names.

The conclusion is that it is possible for a sub-agent to be liable to the principal in negligence for pure economic loss, but that this will depend on there being a duty of care of the kind first recognised by the House of Lords in *Hedley Byrne v Heller*. This is only likely to arise in a limited range of circumstances. The broader approach suggested by *Junior Books v Veitchi* has not been revived by the decision in *Henderson v Merrett*.

The relationship between sub-agent, agent, and principal, was considered further in *Aiken v Stewart Wrightson Members' Agency Ltd*,[88] another case arising out of the collapse of the Lloyd's insurance market. The focus here was primarily on the liabilities of the agents (the 'members agents') rather than the sub-agents (the 'managing agents'). Following *Henderson v Merrett*, it was again held that there was a duty of care in tort owed between the managing agents and the Lloyd's names (the principals), despite the fact that there was no contractual relationship between them. More difficulty, however, surrounded the precise liabilities of the members' agents, and in particular whether they owed a duty in tort as well as in contract. This was important on the facts of the case, because there were issues of limitation, which it was argued could operate more favourably in relation to the names if there was liability in tort as opposed to, or in addition to, contract.

---

[88]   [1995] 3 All ER 449.

As regards the members' agents contractual liability, Potter J accepted the view expressed by Saville J at first instance in *Henderson v Merrett*.[89] This was to the effect that the members' agents had a contractual duty to the effect that underwriting would be carried out with due care and skill. This meant that the members agents were contractually responsible for the underwriting activities of their sub-agents, the managing agents. If the managing agents failed to carry out their underwriting work with due care and skill, this would constitute a breach of the members' agents contract with the names. In other words, the terms of the agent's contract with the principal meant that the agent was contractually liable for failures by the sub-agent to act with due care and skill.

The names wished to establish, however, that the members' agents were similarly liable in tort for the activities of the managing agents. This depended on arguing either that the tortious duty owed to the names ought to be construed in the contractual context, and therefore aligned to the contractual duty; or, that the members' agents' duties in relation to the details of the operation of the underwriting business were non-delegable, and that therefore they remained responsible on that basis for negligence by the managing agents.

In relation to the first argument, Potter J relied in part on the speech of Lord Goff in *Henderson v Merrett*. Lord Goff recognised that tortious duties could exist alongside a contract, though the contract could explicitly exclude them. He did not need, however, in that case to determine the precise nature of the tortious duty existing as between a members' agent and a name. The issue was therefore open to decision in the current case. Potter J accepted the members' agents' contention that:

> the practice of Lloyd's, known to all syndicate names, involves the performance of the actual underwriting function by an independent contractor working in the course of his own business and not that of the members' agents.[90]

It followed from this that, the common law duty of care to be imposed on the members' agents was:

> no more than one of reasonable care in the selection of and liaison with the managing agent coupled with general oversight of the members' interests.[91]

---

[89] *Ibid*, at p 457/458.
[90] *Ibid*, at p 463.
[91] *Ibid*, at p 468.

The members' agents were not under any duty (unless put on inquiry for some reason as to the competence of a managing agent) to supervise or interfere managing or controlling of a syndicate's business.[92]

The argument that the members' agents' tortious duty was the same as the contractual duty therefore failed, unless it could be shown that that contractual duty was non-delegable. As to this issue Potter J noted that the general rule is that a person is not liable for the negligence of a properly employed and apparently competent independent contractor. The exceptions which exist, and which may be said to create an 'non-delegable' duty, have generally arisen where the activity concerned is inherently dangerous or hazardous.[93] That was not the case here. Moreover it was well-known to all Lloyd's names that the underwriting itself would be carried out by an independent contractor (the managing agent) rather than the members' agent. In the light of this, and having given careful consideration to two other cases relied on by the plaintiffs (*Rogers v Night Riders (a firm)*,[94] and *Cynat Products Ltd v Landbuild (Investment and Property) Ltd*[95]), Potter J came to the conclusion that the members' agents were entitled to rely on the managing agents to carry out the detailed underwriting work, and owed no duty to the names to carry out any close supervision of this.

In terms of the relationship between principal, agent and sub-agent, the case confirms that in some cases the sub-agent will owe a duty of care direct to the principal. It also shows that delegation of both the carrying out of responsibilities, and tortious liability for negligence in their execution, can take place, provided that the principal is aware of what is happening. It should not be overlooked, however, that the members' agents could not delegate their contractual liability. As has been noted above, although this was not on the facts of the case helpful to the principals (the names),[96] it is in line with the rule that in general the agent's contractual obligations towards the principal may not be delegated to a sub-agent.

---

[92] In reaching these conclusions, Potter J found assistance in the judgment of Le Dain J in the Canadian Supreme Court's decision in *Central Trust Co v Rafuse* (1986) 31 DLR (4th) 481 at pp 521-522.

[93] Eg *Wilsons and Clyde Coal Co Ltd v English* [1937] 3 All ER 628; *Green v Fibreglass Ltd* [1958] 2 All ER 521.

[94] [1983] RTR 324.

[95] [1984] 3 All ER 513.

[96] This was because of the limitation issue.

Fiduciary duties

The relationship of principal and agent is recognised as being fiduciary, perhaps by analogy with the position of a trustee. Whereas a trustee has a power over trust property, held on behalf of another, which requires duties of good faith, the agent has a similar power to affect the legal relations of the principal. The agent may also in some circumstances be entrusted with the principal's property, or receive property (including money) on the principal's behalf. As a result there are some clearly established fiduciary duties which attach to an agent, whether contractual or gratuitous. These may be conveniently considered under the following headings:

- Duty to avoid a conflict of interest;
- Duty not to make a secret profit;
- Duty not to take bribes;
- Duty to account

Before discussing these categories, however, it should be noted that as far as 'commercial agents', within the definition of the Commercial Agents (Council Directive) Regulations 1993,[97] are concerned, a general, non-derogable, duty to act *in good faith* towards the principal, is imposed (reg 3(1)). The duties of commercial agents under these regulations are considered separately later in this chapter.

Duty to avoid a conflict of interest

An obvious example of the possibility of a conflict of interest arises where an agent employed to buy or sell, either buys his own property, or sells to himself. In *Armstrong v Jackson*[98] the plaintiff, who had no business experience, engaged the defendant, who was a stockbroker, to buy shares in a certain company. The defendant in fact sold his own shares to the plaintiff. When the plaintiff discovered this, he brought an action to rescind the contract. It was held that he was entitled to do so. As McCardie J pointed out, there was a clear conflict of interest:

> [A] broker who secretly sells his own shares is in a wholly false position. As vendor it is in his interest to sell his shares at the highest price. As broker it is his clear duty to the principal to buy at the lowest price and to give unbiased and independent advice (if such be asked) as to the time when and the price at which shares shall be bought, or whether they shall be bought at all.

---

[97] The background to these regulations, and the definition of 'commercial agent' are discussed in Chapter 1, at p 13.

[98] [1917] 2 KB 822.

Moreover the bar, which existed at the time,[99] to rescinding an executed contract for innocent misrepresentation did not apply where there was a fiduciary relationship between the parties. The alternative remedy for the principal (which would have to be used if rescission were not available as a result of affirmation, lapse of time, or third party involvement), is to recover any profit that the agent has made on the transaction.

The burden of proof rests on the agent. In other words, the agent has to prove that there was no conflict of interest in such a situation,[100] otherwise it will be presumed that there was, and the principal will be able to take the appropriate remedies. Alternatively, the agent may be able to show that the principal had full knowledge of the potential for conflict, but still continued with the transaction. Thus in *Harrods Ltd v Lemon*[101] the defendant employed the plaintiffs' estate agency department to find a buyer for her house. They found C, who was prepared to buy 'subject to survey'. C engaged the plaintiffs' surveying department. It was found that the drains were in need of repair. When C told the defendant this, she was annoyed to learn of the plaintiffs' involvement, but eventually sold the house to C at a reduced price. She refused, however, to pay the plaintiffs their commission, relying on the conflict of interest. It was held that the plaintiffs were entitled to their commission. Although there was a clear conflict of interest, and a breach of duty on the part of the plaintiffs, once the defendant knew the full facts of the situation she continued with the contract, and therefore was liable to pay.

Disclosure, therefore, does not have to be made at the outset. Provided that the principal knows the truth before irrevocable commitments are made, the agent will be protected.

Duty not to make a secret profit

An agent may not use his or her position as agent for personal gain, unless the principal has knowledge of this, and is agreeable to it. If such a gain is made, the agent will hold it on trust for the principal, and will have to account to the principal for it. It may also amount to a breach of duty sufficient to entitle the principal to refuse to pay commission or to dismiss the agent.

---

[99] But which does not do so any longer, by virtue of s 1 Misrepresentation Act 1967.

[100] *Collins v Hare* (1828) 2 Bli (NS) 106: *Allison v Clayhills* (1907) 97 LT 709.

[101] [1931] 2 KB 157.

The classic statement of this rule is to be found in the *dicta* of Lord Denning MR in the Court of Appeal in *Boardman v Phipps*:[102]

> It is quite clear that if an agent uses *property*, with which he has been entrusted by his principal, so as to make a profit for himself out of it, without his principal's consent, then he is accountable for it to his principal ... So, also, if he uses a *position of authority*, to which he has been appointed by his principal, so as to gain money for himself, then he is also accountable to his principal for it ... Likewise with *information or knowledge* which he has been employed by his principal to collect or discover, *or which he has otherwise acquired*, for the use of his principal, then again if he turns it to his own use, so as to make a profit by means of it for himself, he is accountable.

There are thus three ways in which the agent may act to make such a secret profit, namely, (i) use of property, (ii) use of position, (iii) use of information or knowledge.

Use of property

One of the easiest ways in which the agent may derive a secret benefit from the principal's property is where the agent is given money for some purpose by the principal, and the agent invests this, retaining any interest earned. There is a duty to hand the interest over to the principal.[103] The same situation may result from the treatment of the proceeds of the sale of the principal's property. In *Burdick v Garrick*[104] the agent was held liable to pay interest on the proceeds of such a sale which had been paid into the agent's firm's account. The property does not, of course, have to be money. An agent who, unable to find a cargo for the principal's ship, loads it with his own goods, is liable to account for the profit made on the sale of the cargo.[105] And an agent who, without authorisation, uses the principal's telegraph system for the transmission of private messages is liable to account for any profits resulting from such use.[106]

---

[102] [1965] Ch 992 at 1018–9. Note that Bowstead mistakenly attributes this *dictum* to Pearson LJ.

[103] *Brown v IRC* [1965] AC 244. This case concerned solicitors holding client's money: the position in relation to this is now governed by statute, namely the Solicitors' Act 1974 s 37.

[104] (1870) LR 5 Ch App 233.

[105] *Shallcross v Oldham* (1862) 2 Johns & H 609.

[106] *Reid-Newfoundland Co v Anglo-American Telegraph Co Ltd* [1912] AC 555.

Use of position

In some circumstances an agent can gain an advantage simply through the fact that they are in the position of agent. In *Turnbull v Garden*[107] the agent was asked to obtain goods for the principal. He did so, but managed to obtain a discount from the supplier on the purchase. He nevertheless sought to recover the full price from the principal. It was held that he was not entitled to do so, since this would amount to a secret profit. Indeed, in certain circumstances, the failure to disclose or pass on a discount of this kind could amount to a bribe (see the next section). This was not the case in *Turnbull v Garden*, but the agent was nevertheless not allowed to gain a secret advantage from being put in the position of agent.[108]

The case cited by Lord Denning in *Boardman v Phipps*[109] as authority in relation to the agent's misuse of their position was *Reading v Attorney General*.[110] This concerned an army sergeant who, while stationed in Cairo, had received money for assisting civilian lorries carrying illicit goods to avoid inspection by the police. The money was seized by the military authorities. The sergeant sought to recover it, but it was held that since the sergeant had acquired it as a result of the misuse of his position as an agent of the Crown, he could not do so. Bowstead doubts whether this case was appropriate for the use of agency principles,[111] and it might well be argued that the criminal nature of the sergeant's actions distinguishes this case from others in this category. Indeed, it might well have been more properly considered as a 'bribe' (see the following section).

Many of the cases in this category involve company directors, using contacts made as agents of the company in order to enter into personally beneficial transactions. A typical example is *Industrial Development Consultants v Cooley*.[112] The plaintiff company's managing director was negotiating a contract with a third party, on behalf of the company. The third party indicated that he would not contract with the company, but would contract with the managing director personally. The managing director thereupon resigned from the company on spurious grounds, and then entered into the contract. It was held that he was liable to account to the company for his profits. Although the company could not have made the contract (because the third party was not willing to deal

---

[107] (1869) 38 LJ Ch 331.

[108] See also *Thompson v Meade* (1891) 7 TLR 698.

[109] See above, note 88, and accompanying text.

[110] [1951] AC 507.

[111] *Op cit*, p 185, n 55.

[112] [1972] 1 WLR 443.

with it), the managing director had broken his fiduciary duty by taking advantage of his position as agent of the company to make a personal gain.[113] It must be remembered, however, that the prohibition is against *secret* profits. If the agent makes full disclosure to the principal before entering into the transaction, there will be no breach of duty, and no liability.[114]

Use of information or knowledge

There may well be some overlap between this category and the previous one. The agent who acquires information in the course of the agency, and uses it for personal gain, may be said to be taking advantage of the position of agent. The previous category is broader, however, and the cases concerned with the misuse of information and knowledge have sufficient peculiarity for it to be justifiable to treat them separately. As far as 'commercial agents' within the meaning of the Commercial Agents (Council Directive) Regulations 1993,[115] are concerned there is a specific duty on the agent to 'communicate to his principal all the necessary information available to him' (reg 3(2)(b)).

The relevant principle under the common law was stated by Lindley LJ in *Lamb v Evans*[116] in the following terms: '[A]n agent has no right to employ as against his principal materials which the agent has obtained only for his principal and in the course of his agency.' The relevant 'materials' in this case consisted of information about traders to be inserted in a directory. Canvassers who, as agents of the plaintiff, had collected this information, could be restrained from using it in a rival publication. Similarly in *Peter Pan Manufacturing Corporation v Corsets Silhouette Ltd*[117] the dispute was about information acquired by the agents in confidence, in this case directly from the principal. The information concerned new designs for brassières, which the agents, who were licensees for existing products, made use of in creating their own products. They terminated their licence arrangements, and sold the new products in competition with the principal. It was held that the principal was entitled to an injunction to restrain further sale, and an account of profits.

---

[113] See also *Cook v Deeks* [1916] 1 AC 554; *Regal (Hastings) Ltd v Gulliver* [1967] 2 AC 134n.

[114] See, for example, the Australian case of *Queensland Mines Ltd v Hudson* (1978) 52 AJLR 399 (PC).

[115] The background to these regulations, and the definition of 'commercial agent' contained in them are discussed in Chapter 1, at p 13.

[116] [1893] 1 Ch 218.

[117] [1963] 3 All ER 402.

The high-watermark of an agent's responsibility in this area is probably to be found in *Boardman v Phipps*.[118] Here the agent had made use of information about the value of shares in a private company. This had been obtained while acting as solicitor for a trust which included a shareholding in the company. As part of a scheme intended to protect the best interests of the trust, the agent purchased shares in the company with his own money. Full disclosure was made to some of the trustees, but not all. It was held by the House of Lords that the agent was accountable to the trust for the profit made on the share transactions. The reasoning behind this appears to be that the use of this information was the equivalent of using the principal's property. As Lord Denning put it in the Court of Appeal:[119] 'Once it is found that the agent has used his principal's property or his position so as to make money for himself, it matters not that the principal has lost no profits or suffered no damage.'The agent must account 'simply because it is money which the agent ought not to be allowed to keep. He gained an unjust benefit by the use of the principal's property or his position, and must account for it.' The fact that the agent may be attempting to act for the benefit of the principal is irrelevant. The requirement for the agent to disgorge any personal profit may be harsh in some cases, but as Pearson LJ, again in the Court of Appeal, put it:[120] 'The rule of equity is rigid. The agent who has made a profit from his agency, without having obtained informed consent from his principal, has to account for the whole of the profit.'

Duty not to take bribes

The reason for this prohibition is obvious – a bribed agent cannot be expected to put the interests of his or her principal first. A 'bribe' is, however, given a broad definition in this context, as is shown by the case of *Industries & General Mortgage Co Ltd v Lewis*.[121] L employed V as an agent to obtain a loan. V obtained one through I&GM. L paid I&GM a fee for obtaining the loan, but, unknown to him, I&GM paid part of this fee to V. I&GM did not know that L was unaware of what had been done. It was nevertheless held that the payment to V was a bribe, and therefore recoverable by L. Slade J ruled that as far as the civil law is concerned a bribe simply means the payment of a secret commission, and there are only three necessary requirements:

- a payment made to the agent;
- the third party who makes the payment is aware that the agent is acting as an agent;

---

[118] [1967] 2 AC 46.
[119] [1965] Ch 992, at p 1019.
[120] *Ibid*, at p 1030.
[121] [1949] 2 All ER 573.

- the third party fails to disclose to the principal that the payment has been made to the agent.[122]

On this basis, where there is a secret payment to an agent, there is, in effect an irrebuttable presumption that the payer acted corruptly, that the agent has been influenced, and that the principal has suffered a loss. A slightly narrower approach was taken, however, by Leggatt J in *Anangel Atlas Compania Naviera SA v Ishikawijama-Harima Heavy Industries Co Ltd*.[123] He suggested, much along the same lines as Slade J, that a bribe:[124] 'consists in a commission or other inducement, which is given by a third party to an agent as such, and which is secret from the principal.' He then went on to state, however, that the 'key to the determination' of whether such payment or inducement is a bribe is: 'whether or not the making of it gives rise to a conflict of interest, that is to say, puts the agent into a position where his duty and his interest conflict.'

This adds to the Slade definition a requirement of conflict of interest. It remains to be seen whether this will be taken up in later cases as something the principal must prove, in addition to the making of a secret payment. In truth, it is likely to be a requirement that is easy to satisfy. If the agent is receiving benefits from the third party, without the principal's knowledge, it is likely that they are not fully representing the principal's interests in the transaction.

Once it has been established that a bribe, within the above definitions, has been paid, the principal has very powerful remedies available. The agent is, in breach of duty and can be dismissed. The principal may, in addition, recover (from either the agent or the third party) either the amount of the bribe or the amount of any loss suffered. This loss may be calculated in terms of any gain acquired by the third party. Thus in *Mahesan v Malaysia Government Officers' Co-operative Housing Society Ltd*[125] the agent had been paid a bribe of $122,000, being one quarter of the profit of $488,000 which the third party made on the transaction. It was held that the principal was entitled to recover from the agent either the amount of the bribe (a restitutionary remedy), or the amount of the profit (in the tort of deceit, or conspiracy). The third party was in this case unavailable, but the liability in relation to the action for deceit is joint and several as between the agent and the third party. The Privy Council in this case, however, rejected earlier authorities[126] which

---

[122] *Ibid*, at p 575.

[123] [1990] 1 Lloyd's Rep 167.

[124] *Ibid*, at p 171.

[125] [1979] AC 374.

[126] Eg *Salford Corporation v Lever* [1891] 1 QB 168.

suggested that the principal could recover both the bribe, and the amount of any loss. It was thought that this would allow for double recovery by the principal, and it is now established that the principal must choose, at least before judgment, which of the two remedies to pursue. The decision will be likely to depend on the respective amounts involved, and on the availability and solvency of the potential defendants.

In *Attorney General for Hong Kong v Reid*,[127] the Privy Council again considered the consequences of the taking of a bribe by a fiduciary. It was held that the recipient should be regarded as a trustee of the bribe. Thus, if the property which constitutes or represents the bribe increases in value, the principal is entitled to claim the full value, on the basis of a constructive trust. In *Reid* the fiduciary, who was a public prosecutor, and therefore a Crown Servant, had invested money received as bribes in various freehold properties. It was held that the Crown had a proprietary interest in these properties. In reaching this conclusion, the Privy Council made it clear that it considered that the same principles would apply to other fiduciaries, including agents. The principal is, by virtue of this decision, given the power to both 'trace' money given as a bribe into other property which may have been purchased with it, and to recover the full value of the relevant property at the time when the agent is compelled to disgorge the bribe.

It should be noted that a situation involving a bribe may well also give rise to criminal liability for conspiracy to defraud, or under the Prevention of Corruption Act 1916.

Duty to account

There are two aspects to this duty. The first is the obligation on the agent to keep proper accounts of their dealings with the principal. In particular there is an obligation to keep the principal's property separate.[128] In the absence of this, presumptions will operate against the agent, as to the ownership of property, or the records of transactions.

The second aspect of this duty is the obligation enforceable by the equitable action of account. This is essentially an action of discovery, whereby the agent can be compelled to disclose and account for all transactions undertaken on the principal's behalf. It may be appropriate where it is unclear exactly what has been paid or transferred to the agent. As Bowstead comments, however,[129] the process is likely to be 'a

---

[127] [1994] 1 All ER 1.
[128] *Gray v Haig* (1855) 20 Beav 219.
[129] *Op cit*, p 195.

long and complex matter', and therefore not to be embarked on lightly. In some cases, however, it may be the only way for the principal to discover the true position, and may assist them in enforcing the other duties noted in this section.

The duty to account was recently considered by Colman J in *Yasuda Fire and Marine Insurance Co of Europe Ltd v Orion Marine Insurance Underwriting Agency Ltd*.[130] The issue in this case was the extent to which the agent (an underwriting agency) was obliged to provide access to its records to the principal. Some of the areas of dispute here related to the facts that the records were held on computer, and that the principal was seeking access to information after the termination of the agency relationship. These matters are discussed in Chapter 6.[131] In the course of considering these aspects of the case, however, Colman J expressed some views on the more general obligation to keep accounts, and provide records. He summarised the position as follows:[132]

> That obligation to provide an accurate account in the fullest sense arises by reason of the fact that the agent has been entrusted with the authority to bind the principal to transactions with third parties and the principal is entitled to know what his personal contractual rights and duties are in relation to those third parties, as well as what he is entitled to receive by way of payment from the agent.

There are thus two reasons for requiring the agent to keep and provide accounts. The first is that the principal is, by virtue of the agency relationship, deemed to be a party to the transactions entered into in the principal's name by the agent with third parties. It is only right that as a participant in those transactions the principal should be entitled to records of them. Only by receiving this information will the principal be fully apprised of the rights and obligations which exist *vis-à-vis* third parties. Secondly, as regards the relationship between the principal and agent, this information will enable the principal to check that the agent is passing on the correct amounts flowing from such transactions.

A further consequence of the provision of accounts, will be that the principal will be able to calculate properly any commission, or other payment, due to the agent. It was emphasised in this case, however, that the duty to account was not dependent on the agency being contractual. Colman J was unable to find any authority suggesting that the same duty did not apply to gratuitous agents. If the agency is contractual, then it is possible for the principal and agent to agree that the duties outlined above should be amended or replaced. In the absence of specific agreement to this effect, however, the law will imply the duty both to

---

[130] [1995] 3 All ER 211.
[131] At p 155.
[132] [1995] 3 All ER 211, at p 219.

keep accounts, and to provide the principal with records of transactions.[133] In the present case, the duty was amended, to the extent that the principal was given a right of inspection, rather than the agent being under a duty to provide records. Apart from this, however, the duty on the agent had not been excluded by the contract. It is clear, therefore, that principals and agents who do wish to operate on a basis different from that implied by law in this area, will have to do so explicitly and unambiguously.

DUTIES OF COMMERCIAL AGENTS

Part II of the Commercial Agents (Council Directive) Regulations 1993[134] set out the rights and obligations of both agents and principals. As far as an agent's duties are concerned, these are contained in reg 3. By virtue of reg 5(1) the parties may not derogate from these.

The basic duty of the commercial agent is stated to be to 'look after the interests of his principal and act dutifully and in good faith'.[135] This very general statement is then expanded a little in reg 3(2), where it is stated that:

In particular, a commercial agent must –

(a) make proper efforts to negotiate and, where appropriate, conclude the transactions he is instructed to take care of;

(b) communicate to his principal all the necessary information available to him;

(c) comply with reasonable instructions given by his principal.

To a large extent, these duties may be said to have their parallels in the common law duties which we have considered in the earlier part of this chapter. There are some ways, however, in which the duties contained in these regulations may extend further than, or operate differently to, the common law, and so each of them will be looked at in turn.

General duties

Regulation 3(1) contains general duties, which are then partially, but not comprehensively, defined in reg 3(2). The first of these general duties is

---

[133] *Ibid*, at p 220.
[134] See above, p 13.
[135] Regulation 3(1).

to 'look after' the principal's interests. This can obviously be related to the common law obligation to avoid conflicts of interest.[136] An agent who gets into a situation where there is such a conflict clearly could not be said to be looking after the principal's interests. It is not clear to what extent this duty is intended to be a 'pro-active' one, so that a commercial agent could be said to have a duty to explore new markets, or look out for new opportunities for business, on behalf of the principal. It seems unlikely that English courts would impose any such obligation on an agent, unless this was specifically part of the agent's agreed responsibilities. In other words, the onus is likely to remain on the principal to specify that the agent is to engage in such activities, if that is what the principal expects.

The other general duty in reg 3(1) is to 'act dutifully and in good faith'. The phrase 'act dutifully' seems virtually meaningless. Clearly agents must act in accordance with their duties, but the obligation to do so arises from the definition of a duty, and so the specific obligation stated here is redundant, other than simply as a reinforcement of what is already the case. The second part of this duty, ie to act 'in good faith', has more possibility of substance. General duties of good faith are, however, an unfamiliar concept in English commercial law, and this obligation reflects the origins of the Regulations in an European Directive. In giving content to it, no doubt English courts will start from the particular fiduciary duties which are well-established in the common law, and have been dealt with above. Rules against the making of secret profits, or gaining private advantage from the use of information or position arising from the agency relationship, are specific examples of a good faith duty. Whether the courts will feel able to extend the law beyond these established categories is open to question. In particular, it may be difficult to argue for a positive duty of this kind, rather than the negative duty 'not to act in bad faith', which seems a more accurate description of the current common law rules.

Specific duties

The first of these is to 'make proper efforts' to negotiate and conclude transactions falling within the agents' instructions.[137] Note that this goes beyond the duty to obey instructions (which is dealt with in reg 3(2)(c)). In effect, it amounts to an obligation of due diligence. The agent will be required to take reasonable steps towards completing transactions. The agent who is lazy and fails to act in such a way will not only run the risk

---

[136] Above, p 60.
[137] Regulation 3(2)(a).

of losing commission, but will also be in breach of duty, with the possibility of the principal being entitled to terminate the agency on this basis. This duty has no parallel in the common law rules applying to agents.

The second specific duty is to communicate 'all the necessary information available to him' to the principal.[138] As we have seen, the common law imposes a fiduciary duty not to make secret gain from information acquired while acting as an agent.[139] The common law does not, however, impose any general obligation to communicate information to the principal, which is what this regulation does. It would clearly not be reasonable, to expect the agent to pass on every item of information acquired. The regulation therefore qualifies the duty by the word 'necessary'. The regulation does not specify what this means in this context. It must be taken to mean, however, information which any reasonable agent would realise that it was necessary for the principal to have in order to carry out effectively the business they are engaged in. Information about the movement (or likely movement) of the market price of goods, about the development of new markets, or about the activities of competing businesses, might all fall into this category.

The final specific obligation is to 'comply with reasonable instructions'.[140] This adds little to the common law obligation to obey instructions, except that it explicitly states that such obedience is only required where the instructions are reasonable. This limitation is almost certainly implicit in the common law rule.

OBLIGATIONS OF THE PRINCIPAL

This section will be shorter than the one which dealt with the powers and obligations of the agent. While there is well-established law defining many aspects of the responsibilities of the agent, there is much less dealing with the obligations of the principal. For that reason, most issues in this area depend on the terms of any agreement as between agent and principal. In particular, if there is a contract governing the relationship, the courts will view their task as simply to interpret that agreement in order to discover the principal's obligations. If the agreement is silent on a particular issue, then no obligation will exist. It is difficult even to find examples of implied terms in this context. For those drafting agreements on behalf of agents, therefore, the advice must be to make sure that

---

[138] Regulation 3(2)(b).

[139] *Boardman v Phipps* [1967] 2 AC 46; see above, p 65.

[140] Regulation (2)(c).

everything is explicit, and that the duties of the principal are clearly spelt out.

The one exception to this general principle that the agreement will determine the obligations occurs in relation to 'commercial agents', as defined by the Commercial Agents (Council Directive) Regulations 1993.[141] These regulations, implementing a European Directive, impose, *inter alia*, a non-derogable obligation on the principal to act in good faith towards a commercial agent. They also contain fairly detailed provisions relating to remuneration. Because they are therefore not in line with the general common law rules relating to the obligations of a principal, and only apply to a particular type of agent, they will be discussed separately towards the end of this chapter.[142] What follows will thus not necessarily apply to commercial agents (as defined in the regulations). In areas where the regulations are silent the common law will continue to operate, but it will be superseded in relation to matters covered by the regulations. In relation to commercial agents, therefore, it will be necessary to take account of both the common law and the regulations.

The main areas of dispute between principal and agent as to the principal's obligations relate to issues of payment. First there is the question of whether the agent who has done what has been requested is entitled to commission, or some other payment, and if so, how much. Second, there may be questions of the reimbursement of expenses, or an indemnity for liabilities incurred in the course of the agency.

Payment of commission

Entitlement

The first issue to be settled is whether the agent is entitled to any payment at all. Some agents may act gratuitously, without the expectation of payment, but nevertheless incurring certain obligations towards the principal.[143] More commonly, there will be an expectation of payment. Here, as elsewhere, however, it is as well to be specific. In *Taylor v Brewer*,[144] for example, the defendants employed an agent 'in going backwards and forwards upon their business', which was the sale of lottery tickets. The defendants later resolved that 'any service to be rendered by [the agent] after the third lottery be taken in to consideration, and such remuneration be made as shall be deemed

---

[141] These regulations, and the definition of 'commercial agent', are discussed in Chapter 1, at p 13.

[142] Below, p 83.

[143] See, for example, *Chaudry v Prabhakar* [1988] 3 All ER 718, above, p 52.

[144] (1813) 1 M&S 290.

right'. The agent claimed that this entitled him to reasonable remuneration. It was held, however, that it was up to the defendants to decide if any payment was due, and if so, how much. The agent had no claim to any remuneration as of right.

Where the agreement specifies that if certain circumstances arise payment is to be made on a particular basis, this will generally be taken to be exclusive, so that it will not be possible to argue that it leaves open the possibility of some other basis for payment in other circumstances. In *John Meacock v Abrahams*,[145] for example, A held a second mortgage over houses owned by L. A instructed the plaintiff auctioneers to sell the houses by auction. The contract included the provision that commission was payable 'if a sale of the property, whether arranged by the auctioneer or not, is effected between the date of acceptance of instructions and the date of the auction'. Before the auction could take place, L sold the houses, and the plaintiffs claimed their commission from A. It was held by the Court of Appeal that the above provision only applied where the sale was by the person who had arranged the auction.[146] Moreover, the plaintiffs were not entitled to a *quantum meruit* payment for the work they had done. Where an agreement deals with the question of remuneration, there is no room for an implied promise to pay a reasonable sum.

If the agreement is silent on the issue, the agent may then be in a stronger position. Provided it can be shown that the agent had not intended to act gratuitously, the courts may well be prepared to hold that 'reasonable' payment was intended. This was the view of the House of Lords in *Way v Latilla*.[147] The appellant had done work in relation to mining concessions in West Africa on behalf of the respondents, but there had never been any clear agreement as to payment. Since the work was clearly not intended to be done gratuitously, the House of Lords held that reasonable payment should be made. They held, in effect, that a term should be implied to this effect. Comparison can be made with s 15 of the Supply of Goods and Services Act 1982, which states that where, in a contract for the supply of a service, the consideration to be paid is not fixed by the contract, 'there is an implied term that the party contracting with the supplier will pay a reasonable charge'. What is a reasonable charge is a question of fact.[148] That question may be informed (but not concluded) by evidence as to the 'going rate' which a professional person would charge for services of

---

[145] [1956] 3 All ER 660.
[146] Morris LJ dissented on this point.
[147] [1937] 3 All ER 759.
[148] Section 15(2).

the kind in question.[149] *A fortiori* if the agreement between principal and agent specifically provides for 'reasonable' remuneration, the courts will have no hesitation is deciding what this should be. If, however, the agreement leaves the discretion as to payment entirely in the hands of the principal, the courts will be reluctant to intervene. In *Kofi Sunkersette Obu v Strauss & Co Ltd*[150] Clause 6 of the agreement between the parties stated:

> The company has agreed to remunerate my services with a monthly sum of fifty pounds to cover my ... expenses for the time being ... A commission is also to be paid to me by the company which I have agreed to leave to the discretion of the company.[151]

The agent argued that the agreement was clearly not intended to be gratuitous, and that, on the basis of *Way v Latilla*, he should be entitled to some reasonable commission in addition to the £50 per month. The Privy Council refused to contemplate this. As Sir John Beaumont put it:[152]

> In their Lordships' opinion the relief which the appellant claims, namely, an account and payment of commission based on rubber purchased or shipped, is beyond the competence of any court to grant. The court cannot determine the basis and rate of the commission. To do so would involve not only making a new agreement for the parties but varying the existing agreement by transferring to the court the exercise of a discretion vested in the respondents.

The lesson from these cases for those drafting a contract for an agent is that if reference is to be made to payment it should always be clear and specific. If there is any ambiguity there is no guarantee that a court will determine it in favour of the agent; indeed, on the contrary, vagueness may well be taken to mean that the agent has no right to remuneration at all. Ironically, the agent may well be in a better position if there is no reference to payment at all, provided that the context is clearly commercial.[153] The insertion of precise terms dealing with payment is, however, obviously the preferred course.

---

[149] *Upsdell v Stewart* (1793) Peake 255. See further Bowstead, *op cit*, pp 211-12, and the cases cited there.

[150] [1951] AC 243.

[151] *Ibid*, at p 249.

[152] *Ibid*, at p 250.

[153] As shown by *Way v Latilla*, above, n 147.

When earned

Once it is established that the agent has a right to payment under the agency agreement, the question may then arise as to when precisely the payment is earned. Once again, the terms of the agreement between the principal and agent will be crucial. Much of the case law in this area is concerned with estate agents, but there is no reason to think that the principles employed are not of more general application.

If the agreement states that payment is to be made on the occurrence of a particular event, eg the sale of a house, then once this has taken place, the agent may well be able to claim commission, irrespective of the agent's contribution to the sale. This type of situation which may lead to a principal having to pay commission to two agents in respect of the same transaction. This is what occurred in *Barnard Marcus & Co v Ashraf*.[154] The defendant was very anxious to sell a property, which he had placed with estate agents. Following some abortive attempts to sell, he then placed it with auctioneers, whose contract provided that commission would be payable if the property was sold after the receipt of instructions, whether the sale was arranged by the auctioneers or not. In fact the property was sold by the original estate agents. The defendant tried to argue that this sale amounted to a withdrawal of the property from the market, which, under the contract with the auctioneers, would have meant that they would only be able to claim expenses. The Court of Appeal, however, decided that the defendant was in fact liable to pay commission to both the estate agents and the auctioneers.

More commonly, however, a dispute between two agents will be decided by asking which one was the 'effective cause' of the sale.[155] This issue is discussed below. First we look at the more general question of how the courts go about determining whether the agent has earned commission.

The leading authority on this is the House of Lords decision in *Luxor (Eastbourne) Ltd v Cooper*.[156] A company wished to sell some cinemas, and Cooper agreed to try to provide a purchaser. The agreement stated that he was to be paid a procuration fee of £10,000 'on completion of the sale'. Cooper provided a willing purchaser, but the company decided not to go through with the sale. Cooper sued for his commission. The House of Lords held that everything turned on the express terms of the contract between Cooper and the company. They were not prepared to imply a term that the principal would not unreasonably prevent the completion of the transaction, since this would be too uncertain. Since

---

[154] [1988] 18 EG 67.
[155] As in, for example, *Bentley's Estate Agents Ltd v Granix Ltd* [1989] 27 EG 93.
[156] [1941] AC 108.

the express terms referred to 'completion of the sale' and this had not taken place, Cooper was not entitled to any commission. If an agent wants to place restrictions over the principal's power to withdraw, this must be express.

An alternative to limiting the principal's power to withdraw is to define the agent's obligations more broadly. The effectiveness of this approach is confirmed by *Christie Owen & Davies v Rapacioli*.[157] The defendant instructed the plaintiffs, who were estate agents, to assist in the sale of the lease and goodwill of a restaurant. It was agreed that the plaintiffs would be entitled to commission if they effected 'an introduction either directly or indirectly of a person ready able and willing to purchase' at £20,000 or any price acceptable to the defendant. The plaintiffs introduced A, who offered £17,700. The defendant agreed to accept this, and a contract was drawn up and signed by A. At this point the defendant, who had had a better offer, withdrew from the transaction. The plaintiffs sued for their commission. The facts were clearly very similar to those of *Luxor v Cooper*.[158] The difference here was that the event which triggered the right to commission was not stated to be the sale of the restaurant, but the introduction of a willing purchaser. The Court of Appeal thus held that provided that an offer to purchase had been made which was within the authorised terms, and that it had not been withdrawn by the offeror (but rather, refused by the vendor), then the agent would, on the wording of this agreement be entitled to commission. Since the facts of this case fulfilled these conditions, the plaintiffs succeeded in their action. It is important, however, that the purchaser in a case such as this should have made an offer which is unqualified. If the agreement is 'subject to contract',[159] or subject to some other condition,[160] then the agent is unlikely to succeed.

The reliance on, and application of, the strict terms of the contract, may mean that the agent's claim will fail where the principal has acted in good faith, and there has been no withdrawal, or other deliberate action which would frustrate the agent's right to commission. In *Fairvale Ltd v Sabharwal*,[161] for example, the agent was acting in relation to the auction of a hotel. The hotel failed to reach its reserve at the auction, but afterwards the agent introduced a prospective purchaser, who eventually bought the property. The contract between the agent and principal provided for commission to be payable if a sale was effected

---

[157] [1974] QB 781.

[158] Above, n 156.

[159] As in *Christie, Owen & Davies v Stockton* [1953] 1 WLR 1353.

[160] For example, *AL Wilkinson Ltd v Brown* [1966] 1 WLR 194 – agreement conditional on the purchaser selling his own house.

[161] [1992] 32 EG 51.

within 28 days of the auction. Through no fault of the principal, the sale was not in fact completed until more than 28 days had passed. The Court of Appeal held that since the sale took place outside the time limit, no commission was payable. Nor was there any room here for a *quantum meruit* claim.[162]

Effective cause

As indicated above, one of the tests of the agent's ability to claim commission is whether his or her actions can be said to have been the 'effective cause' of any transaction which results between the principal and third party.[163] Thus the mere introduction of a tenant or purchaser will not be enough, unless the agent can also be said to have actually brought about the letting or sale. As Phillips J put it in *Bentley's Estate Agents v Granix Ltd*,[164] agents 'get paid for results and not for effort'. The 'effective cause' requirement will apply unless the express language of the agency agreement contradicts it. In *Cooper & Co v Fairview Estates (Investments) Ltd*,[165] for example, the agreement stated that commission was payable 'should you introduce a tenant ... who subsequently completes a lease'. The principal argued that there was *always* an implied term that the agent must be at least *an* effective cause, if not *the* effective cause of the transaction. The Court of Appeal rejected this, and relied on the clear wording of the commission clause. On the issue of whether, where a requirement of 'effective cause' was implied, it should be *'an'* or *'the'* effective cause, the Court was undecided. Bowstead refers to 'the effective cause.[166] Woolf J in *Cooper*, however, was prepared to accept that in respect of certain commission agreements 'an effective cause' would be sufficient.[167] This has not been picked up in any subsequent decision, and with respect it is submitted that, to the extent that the test is used to decide between the claims of competing agents, the approach of Bowstead is preferable. The application of this can be seen in the later Court of Appeal decision in *Chasen Ryder v Hedges*.[168] The plaintiff, an estate agent, had introduced a prospective purchaser, RW, to the defendant. No offer was made, however, and the defendant instructed other agents. The new agents told RW that planning approval was likely for an extension to the property. RW then made an offer and

---

[162] This is in line with the discussion above concerning whether there is any right to remuneration at all – see above, pp 72–74.

[163] See, eg *Millar, Son & Co v Radford* (1903) TLR.

[164] [1989] 27 EG 93

[165] [1987] 1 EGLR 18.

[166] *Op cit*, Article 59.

[167] [1987] 1 EGLR 18, at p 20.

[168] [1993] 8 EG 119.

bought from the defendant. The plaintiffs sued for their commission. The Court of Appeal held that the burden was on the plaintiff to show that his introduction was the effective cause of the purchase. An introduction followed by a sale, without intervening events, shifts the burden to the defendant to show that there was some other cause of the transaction. It is not necessary to show that the purchaser's interest had 'evaporated' prior to the second introduction,[169] but on the facts the plaintiff's introduction of RW was the effective cause of nothing. The second introduction did not depend on the first, and it was the second introduction that was the cause of the purchase. If the Court had been looking for merely *an* effective cause, the plaintiff's claim would have been much stronger, and the Court's decision would have been more difficult. In the absence of other authority on the point, it is safest to assume that what is required is that the agent's actions should be *the* effective cause of the transaction.[170]

Amount

The amount of any payment to be made to the agent will generally be determined by the contract. As we have seen,[171] in the situation where payment is clearly anticipated but the amount is not specified, the court may be prepared to allow the recovery of a reasonable sum by way of a *quantum meruit* payment. Otherwise, the strict terms of the agreement will be adhered to.

One issue which has recently arisen for consideration is the position where payment is on the basis of a percentage commission, but the transaction involves a 'part-exchange'. Is the commission to be based purely on the cash part of the transaction, or should a value be placed on the exchanged property as well? In *Connell Estate Agents v Begej*[172] commission was payable on the 'sale' of a house. The transaction arranged took the form of a cash payment of £53,000 together with the transfer of another house valued at £56,000. The agent claimed commission on £109,000, but the principal was only prepared to pay it on the £53,000. The Court of Appeal held that the transaction was a 'sale' within the meaning of the commission agreement. The 'purchase price' included the value of the transferred house and the agent was therefore titled to commission on the full £109,000.

---

[169] *Cf John Wood v Dantata* [1987] EGLR 23.

[170] See also *Bentley's Estate Agents Ltd v Granix Ltd* [1989] 27 EG 93.

[171] *Way v Latilla* [1937] 3 All ER 759, above note 000 and accompanying text.

[172] [1993] 39 EG 123.

Indemnity

An agent may well incur costs in carrying out the principal's instructions. To what extent is the agent entitled to be indemnified for these expenses, in addition to, or in place of, receiving commission, or other remuneration?

If the agent is in business as an agent, and is therefore being paid for the work, general office expenses relating to, for example, correspondence and telephone calls, will not be recoverable unless specifically provided for. It will be assumed that the payment to the agent is intended to cover such costs. Where, however, the agent is not being paid, or incurs exceptional expenses, or expenses are incurred in relation to a transaction which does not take place, then the agent will be taken to be entitled to reimbursement. The point was made, *obiter*, by Martin B, in *Warlow v Harrison*.[173] In discussing property which had been place with an auctioneer, he commented:

> We entertain no doubt that the owner may, at any time before the contract is legally complete, interfere and revoke the auctioneer's authority: but he does so at his peril; and, if the auctioneer has contracted any liability in consequence of his employment and the subsequent revocation or conduct of the owner, he is entitled to be indemnified.

Where the agency is contractual, this right will probably be based on an implied term,[174] and the agent's action will be in contract. If the agency is non-contractual, then the agent will be relying on restitution, in which case the scope for recovery may be more limited. The contractual agent, for example, may be able to recover payments which were made under a moral, rather than a legal obligation. In *Rhodes v Fielder, Jones and Harrison*,[175] for example, a solicitor agent was instructed by his principal (also a solicitor) not to pay fees to counsel who had acted in successful litigation. The agent nevertheless did so, and was held to be entitled to recover the cost of this from the principal, notwithstanding the fact that the barrister would not have had a legally enforceable claim to the payment. A restitutionary action, which would normally be based on the performance of an act requested by the principal, and providing a benefit to the principal, would not provide a remedy in these circumstances.

A further basis on which reimbursement may be available to either contractual or non-contractual agents, is the custom of a particular place

---

[173] (1859) 1 E&E 309, At 317.
[174] See eg Bowstead, *op cit*, p 247.
[175] (1919) 89 LJKB 15.

or market. In *Bayliffe v Butterworth*[176] the principal was held to be bound to reimburse a broker who, following the principal's failure to deliver, had himself bought shares to fulfil a contract with another broker. The custom in Liverpool, where the transaction took place, was that agents assumed personal liability in relation to share transactions with other brokers, and the principal was aware of this.

The agent will not normally be able to recover expenses in relation to unauthorised actions, despite the decision in *Rhodes v Fielder*. Nor will the principal be liable in relation to expenses incurred by the agent's own negligence, or in relation to an illegal transaction.[177]

Where the agency is contractual, it does not matter that the liability incurred by the agent is not one to which the principal could in law have become liable. This is illustrated by *Adams v Morgan & Co*,[178] where the agent became liable to a personal tax on income that would not have applied to the principal, which was a corporation. The payments were nevertheless recoverable from the principal.

Property rights – the agent's lien

The agent who is in dispute with a principal may have a possible weapon in the fact that the principal may have put property into the agent's hands, or the agent may have received property from a third party on behalf of the principal. In these circumstances the agent may be able to claim a lien over the property. This is the right to retain possession of the property (though not to use or dispose of it) until the principal has made good any debt owing to the agent in terms of commission, or reimbursement of expenses, etc. It is an extreme remedy, and it was suggested, *obiter*, by Mustill J in *Compania Financera 'Soleada' SA v Hamoor Tanker Corp Inc (The Borag)*[179] that it should only be available where the principal's conduct is of a 'repudiatory nature'. No doubt it would be difficult for a relationship of principal and agent to survive the exercise of this 'self-help' remedy by the agent, but there does not appear to be any definite limitation of this kind.

Liens may in theory be either particular (relating to a debt that arises in connection with the property being held), or general (relating to any debt owed by the principal to the agent). In practice the courts are reluctant to find that a general lien exists, unless the parties themselves

---

[176] (1847) 1 Exch 425.
[177] See Bowstead, Article 66, p 252.
[178] [1924] 1 KB 751.
[179] [1980] 1 Lloyd's Rep 111, at p 122.

have explicitly provided for this.[180] The rest of the discussion of this topic will therefore concentrate on particular liens.

In order for the lien to arise, the agent must have possession of the property in question. This does not necessarily mean physical possession. Indeed, physical possession is neither necessary nor sufficient in order for a lien to exist. First, it is clear that possession of documents of title may be enough to establish the lien, even if another person has possession of the property itself. Thus in *Re Pavey's Patent Felted Fabric Co*,[181] the agent had received, and paid, bills representing the value of goods. It was held that this entitled the agent to a lien over the goods, as against the liquidator who had taken physical possession of them. In other words, the agent is entitled in such situations to claim 'constructive' possession. This will also apply where either the principal,[182] or the agent,[183] has entrusted the property to the possession of a third party, provided it is clear that it is held on behalf of the agent.

Second, even where the agent does have actual, rather than constructive, possession, this will not be sufficient unless the possession is 'lawful', and is undertaken 'as agent', rather than in some other capacity. Thus, the agent who seizes property which he has acquired on behalf of the principal, but which was supposed, under their agreement, to remain in the possession of a third party, will not be able to claim a lien.[184] The same will apply if the possession is obtained by a misrepresentation.[185] The requirement that the possession is 'as agent' means that property acquired prior to the start of the agency cannot be the subject of this type of lien. Nor can property which is received by the agent in some other capacity than that of agent.[186] Similarly, the lien cannot be used in relation to debts that arose prior to the agency.[187]

Termination of a lien

The simplest way for the lien to end will be for the principal to pay what is owed to the agent. Tender of payment which is unjustifiably refused will similarly terminate the lien.

---

[180] See Bowstead, Article 67, p 256.

[181] (1876) 1 Ch D 631.

[182] *Bryans v Nix* (1839) 4 M&W 775.

[183] *McCombie v Davis* (1805) 7 East 5.

[184] *Taylor v Robinson* (1818) 8 Taunt 648.

[185] *Madden v Kempster* (1807) 1 Camp 12.

[186] *Dixon v Stansfield* (1850) 10 CB 398.

[187] *Houghton v Matthews* (1803) 3 B&P 485.

The agent will also lose the right by conduct which indicates an intention to abandon the lien, or is inconsistent with it. The lien will be regarded as being 'waived'. Voluntarily parting with possession of the property concerned will be likely to be considered such conduct (though as has been noted above, physical possession is not always necessary for the right to exist). Surrender of possession which is involuntary,[188] or is induced by fraud,[189] will not, however, affect the lien. Nor, apparently will surrender of goods to the principal so that they may be sold, and the agent paid from the proceeds.[190] Finally, it seems that surrender of possession accompanied by a specific reservation of the lien will be effective to prevent the lien being lost.[191]

Other examples of waiver include claiming a right to possession of the property concerned on some basis other than the lien,[192] or allowing goods to be taken in execution.[193] In *Boardman v Sill* the defendant refused to hand over brandy stored in his cellar, claiming that he owned it. In fact warehouse rent was owing in respect of it, which would have given rise to a lien. The defendant was taken to have waived this, however. As Lord Ellenborough put it, 'As the brandy had been detained on a different ground, and as no demand of warehouse rent had been made, the defendant must be taken to have waived his lien'. In *Jacobs v Latour* some horses were in the possession of a trainer. The trainer obtained judgment and a writ of execution against the owner of the horse, in relation to debts owed. The horses were sold by the sheriff to the trainer. All though the horses had never left the physical possession of the trainer, this had the effect of destroying any lien held by the trainer, since 'in order to sell, the sheriff must have had possession; but after he had possession from [the trainer], and with his assent, [the trainer's] subsequent possession must have been acquired under the sale, and not by virtue of his lien'.[194] Both of these cases involved a lien arising other than in the course of agency, but the principles applied in them must be taken to be of general application.[195]

---

188 *Dicas v Stockley* (1836) 7 C&P 587.

189 As in eg *Wallace v Woodgate* (1824) R&M.

190 *North Western Bank Ltd v Poynter, Son & Macdonalds* [1895] AC 56 – though this case concerned the position of pledgor/pledgee, rather than principal and agent. Bowstead (*op cit* p 270), however, treats it as authority for the proposition stated in the text.

191 *Caldwell v Sumpters* [1972] Ch 478.

192 *Boardman v Sill* (1808) 1 Campb 410n; followed in *Weeks v Goods* (1859) 6 CBNS 367.

193 *Jacobs v Latour* (1828) 5 Bing 130.

194 *Ibid per* Best CJ, at p 132.

195 They are certainly treated in this way by Bowstead, *op cit*, p 269.

An authorised sub-agent may also maintain a lien against the principal, to the same extent as the agent, but not generally to any greater extent.[196] Where the principal is undisclosed, however, the sub-agent's lien will be the same as would have been available against the agent, had the agent in fact been the principal.[197]

DUTIES OF PRINCIPAL TOWARDS COMMERCIAL AGENTS

The common law duties of a principal towards a commercial agent are modified by Parts II and III and IV of the Commercial Agents (Council Directive) Regulations 1993.[198] Part II is concerned with general duties, Part III with remuneration, and Part IV primarily with duties on termination. In this section only Parts II and III will be discussed: Part IV will be left to Chapter 6, where the common law rules relating to termination of agency are dealt with. It should be noted, however, that the first regulation within Part IV obliges principal and agent to supply each other, on request, a signed written document setting out the terms of the agency contract, including any terms agreed after its initial formation.[199] This documentary evidence of the agreement may of course be helpful in dealing with the obligations contained in Parts II and III.

General duties

The general duties imposed on a principal are set out in reg 4, and mirror those imposed on the commercial agent by reg 3, which have already been considered.[200] Thus, the principal must act 'dutifully and in good faith' in 'his relations with his commercial agent'.[201]

As has been noted above,[202] the concept of a 'good faith' duty is one that is unfamiliar in the commercial context in the common law. As far as a principal is concerned its most likely practical manifestation will be in keeping the agent informed about matters which affect the transaction concerned, so that the principal cannot be said to be taking an unfair

---

[196] *Fisher v Smith* (1878) 4 App Cas 1.

[197] *Mann v Forrester* (1814) 4 Camp 60.

[198] Enacting Council Directive 86/653/EEC. See above, p 13, where the definition of a 'commercial agent for these purposes is also discussed.

[199] Regulation 13(1).

[200] Above, p 69.

[201] Regulation 4(1).

[202] Page 70.

advantage of the agent. This presumably does not, however, require the principal to give the agent commercially sensitive information. If, for example, the agent is engaged to purchase goods which the principal knows can be sold at a substantial profit in a particular market, there is no need for the agent to be told this, even though the agent could personally benefit from the information, or might use it as the basis for seeking a higher commission from the principal.

Some indication of the kind of information which should be supplied in fulfilling the duty to act in good faith is to be found in reg 4(2)(b). This requires the principal to obtain for (and presumably communicate to) the agent 'the information necessary for the performance of the agency contract'. This indicates a requirement to give practical information as to such matters as details of the goods being dealt with, and, possibly, details of prospective buyers or sellers, where the principal has these available. In addition, there is a specific obligation to notify the agent if the volume of transactions appears to be going to be significantly lower than the agent could normally have expected. This must be done within a 'reasonable period' of the principal reaching this conclusion. Thus the principal is not allowed to let the agent turn away other work in anticipation of a large volume of business coming from the principal if the principal knows that this is unlikely to materialise. The final specific obligation as far as communication is concerned is contained in reg 4(3). The principal must, within a reasonable period, inform the agent of action taken in relation to any transaction arranged by the agent. Thus the agent must be notified as to whether the principal has accepted or refused the transaction, or of any 'non-execution' of it. The distinction between 'refusal' and 'non-execution' is not clear. Presumably refusal applies where the transaction does not, in the principal's opinion, fall within the terms of the transactions which the agent has been engaged to undertake. Non-execution would arise where the transaction was within the scope of the agreement, but the principal decided for some other reason not to proceed with it. Both actions might have consequences as regards the agent's remuneration, and also the agent's relationship with the third party with whom the transaction had been negotiated.

A further specific obligation is contained in reg 4(2)(a). This simply states that the principal must 'provide his commercial agent with the necessary documentation relating to the goods concerned'. This appears to be an unexceptional and uncontroversial duty. If the agent is to deal with goods on behalf of the principal, relevant documentation necessary to the transaction must be made available. Where goods are being sold, for example, this might mean documents of title; if goods are being bought from abroad, it may be necessary to provide documentation relating to customs clearance. The exact requirements will, however, vary from transaction to transaction.

The obligations contained in reg 4 are non-derogable.[203] The regulations are, however, silent as to the consequence of breach, other than to say that this shall be governed by 'the law applicable to the contract'.[204] Under English law it seems that likely that the duties will be regarded as being implied terms of the contract between the principal and agent, and that failure to comply will therefore be treated as a breach of contract. The more difficult issues will be, first, establishing whether or not there has been a breach of an obligation (particularly those expressed in very general terms), and, secondly, where such a breach is established, estimating the damages which should follow. Where a failure to notify of an impending reduction in business has caused the agent to reject other commissions then the amount of damages may be fairly easily assessable, but if the breach is of, for example, the general duty to act in good faith, it may be much more difficult to identify an appropriate figure. For this reason agents may well be reluctant to take legal proceedings in respect of this type of breach. If this is so, then it may be questionable whether these parts of the regulations will in practice make any significant difference to the way in which principals treat their agents.

Remuneration

As we have seen, the common law deals with the question of remuneration largely as a matter of construction of the contract between principal and agent. This will govern both the entitlement to commission or other payment, and the amount payable. Regulations 6 to 12 of the Regulations mean that, as far as commercial agents are concerned, the common law approach has been superseded.

Regulation 6 deals with the agent's entitlement to payment. It operates in the absence of any agreement between the parties. The common law approach here may be to say either that no payment is payable in these circumstances,[205] or that a reasonable amount may be claimed.[206] The latter approach is that which is adopted in the Regulations. If there is a custom of the place where the agent 'carries on his activities', then payment should be paid on this customary basis. Otherwise, in the absence of agreement, the agent is entitled to

---

[203] Regulation 5(1).

[204] Regulation 5(2).

[205] As in *Kofi Sunkersette Obu v Strauss & Co Ltd* [1951] AC 243, see above, p 74.

[206] As in *Way v Latilla* [1937] 3 All ER 759, see above, p 73.

'reasonable remuneration'. The regulation is stated to be 'without prejudice to the application of any enactment or rule of law concerning the *level* of remuneration' (emphasis added).[207] It clearly takes precedence, however, over any common law rules as to *entitlement* to remuneration.

Regulations 7 to 12 deal with the situation where the agent is paid (wholly or in part) by commission.[208] The agent is entitled to commission where 'a transaction has been concluded as a result of his action'.[209] It seems likely that this will be interpreted in the light of the common law development of the concept of 'effective cause', which has been discussed above.[210] Regulation 7(1)(b) and 7(2), however, go on to give the agent a right to claim commission on a slightly wider basis. Regulation 7(1)(b) entitles the agent to commission where a transaction 'is concluded with a third party whom he has previously acquired as a customer for transactions of the same kind'. This means that once a customer has been introduced, the fact that the principal may in future deal directly with the customer, and not via the agent, will not preclude the agent claiming commission on the resulting transactions. This right will continue as long as the agency agreement itself subsists.

Regulation 7(2) deals with the situation where an agent has been given an exclusive right in relation to a specific geographical area, or a specific group of customers. Once again, as long as the agency agreement is in existence, the agent will be entitled to commission on all transactions of the relevant type which are entered into by the principal with customers within the specified area or group. This is irrespective of any direct or indirect involvement of the agent with the transaction. It thus acts as a reinforcement of the agent's exclusive right, and discourages the principal from using any other agent, or dealing directly with customers, in the relevant market.

Whereas reg 7 is concerned with transactions concluded during the currency of the agency agreement, reg 8 deals with the position as regards transactions concluded after the termination of the agency. The more straightforward provision is reg 8(b), which provides that where a transaction falls within the scope of those dealt with by reg 7, and the order of the third party was received prior to the termination of the agency, the agent will be entitled to commission. Regulation 8(a) allows the agent to recover commission where a transaction is 'mainly attributable to his efforts during the period covered by the agency

---

[207] Regulation 6(2).
[208] Regulation 6(3).
[209] Regulation 7(1).
[210] See pp 77–78.

contract' provided that 'the transaction was entered into within a reasonable period after the contract terminated'. This leaves considerable scope for dispute. What input will be required from the agent to establish that the transaction was 'mainly attributable' to his or her efforts? Is this any different from the common law test of 'effective cause'?[211] Moreover, where the transaction is attributable to the agent, what will be regarded as a 'reasonable period' following the termination of the agency within which it must have been entered into? The vagueness of the language means that the only way of resolving disputes may be by litigation. Unless and until this provides further guidance on the meaning of these phrases, this may well reduce the effectiveness of these provisions on a day-to-day basis for commercial agents.

Regulation 9 deals with the situation where there may be, as a result of the operation of regulations 7 and 8, a claim for commission by more than one agent. Where one agent has succeeded another, who will be entitled to commission on transactions which have begun under the first agency agreement but are concluded during the currency of the second? The basic rule is that reg 8 overrides reg 7, so that the first agent should recover fully wherever the conditions of reg 8 are satisfied. The regulation provides an exception to this, however, if it is 'equitable because of the circumstances' for the commission to be shared.[212] The most likely situation for this to arise would seem to be where there is a dispute as to whether the transaction is 'mainly attributable' to the efforts of the first or the second agent. Since the possibility of apportionment is specifically recognised by this regulation, parties may well be encouraged to settle disputes in this way, without resorting to litigation. Strictly speaking, reg 9(1) should only operate where the transaction *is* mainly attributable to the first agent, but for some reason the actions of the second agent also justify a share of the commission. If the first agent does not satisfy the 'mainly attributable' condition, then he or she has no claim at all under reg 8(a). It is submitted, however, that the provision in reg 9(1) may well be interpreted in a flexible way, so as to allow more general scope for apportionment.

Where the first agent's claim under reg 8 fails, reg 9 does not automatically mean that the second agent will succeed. It may be that neither agent is entitled to commission on the transaction in question.

---

[211] *Ibid.*
[212] Regulation 9(1).

If the principal has made payment of commission to one agent, and it is determined that the other should have received some or all of it, the relevant amount must be repaid to the principal.[213] The primary obligation as regards repayment is placed on the agent who is receipt of the overpayment. The principal nevertheless remains liable to pay each agent what is due on the basis of the regulations. Thus, if the agent who has been overpaid fails to make a refund to the principal, this will not remove the principal's obligation to pay the other agent what is owed.[214]

Regulation 10 concerns the dates at which commission becomes due, and by which it must be paid. Regulation 10(1) sets out three circumstances, the occurrence of any of which will trigger the right to payment of commission. It is assumed that in referring to 'execution' the regulations mean full performance of the transaction – ie the delivery of and payment for goods, rather than the making of a contract to do so. The three circumstances arise where:

- the principal has executed the transaction; or
- the principal should, according to his agreement with the third party, have executed the transaction; or
- the third party has executed the transaction.

At the latest commission becomes due when event (c) has occurred, or should have occurred 'if the principal had executed his part of the transaction'.[215] The parties are not allowed to alter this provision by their agreement, in a way that operates to the detriment of the agent.[216] To this extent, therefore, the freedom of the principal and agent to determine their own obligations as to the payment of commission is removed.

The same is true of the date for payment, which is dealt with by reg 10(3). This sets the latest date for payment as the last day of the month following the quarter in which it became due. In calculating the quarters, the regulation provides that:

> unless otherwise agreed between the parties, the first quarter period shall run from the date the agency contract takes effect, and subsequent periods shall run from that date in the third month thereafter or the beginning of the fourth month, whichever is the sooner.

These provisions are not very clear, but it is submitted that their effect is as follows. If the agency agreement takes effect on the 5 January,

---

[213] Regulation 9(2).
[214] *Ibid.*
[215] Regulation 10(2).
[216] Regulation 10(4).

the next quarter will start on 5 April. Any payments which became due between 5 January and 4 April will be payable on 30 April. If the agency takes effect on 31 March, since there is no 31 June, the next quarter will start on 1 July. Payments falling due between 31 March and 30 June will be payable on the 31 July.

Two issues remain unclear. In the example just given, where the agency starts on the 31 March, and the second quarter starts on 1 July, the third quarter must start on 1 October (as again there is no 31 September). But should the fourth quarter start on 31 December, or 1 January? Secondly, if the agency starts on 31 December, the second quarter will start on 31 March. What is the last date for payment for commission falling due between 31 December and 30 March? Is it 31 March or 30 April? It is submitted that 31 March is the right date, but a case could be made for either on the basis of the wording of the regulation. These uncertainties mean that principals and agents will be well-advised either to avoid starting their agreements on the 31 of any month, or (and this may be the safest course) should spell out precisely in the agreement when the quarters are going to run.

The regulations so far discussed have dealt with the ways in which commission is payable. Regulation 11 recognises that in limited circumstances the right to commission may be lost. Only one event will extinguish the right to commission: the non-execution of the contract between the principal and third party.[217] Once it is established that the contract will not take place, and that this for a reason 'for which the principal is not to blame',[218] then the right to commission will be extinguished. As with reg 10, the parties may not agree to any alternative to this which might operate to the detriment of the agent. Any such agreement to derogate will be void.[219] They may, however, make a valid agreement which is more advantageous to the agent.

The circumstances where commission will be lost will thus include:

- the third party's withdrawal from the contract;
- the frustration of the contract;
- action by the agent which means that the contract does not proceed.

The use of the concept of 'blame' is unusual in English contract law, as Reynolds has pointed out.[220] It gives rise to uncertainty in relation to some situations. If the principal has innocently attached an incorrect description to goods being sold, the third party buyer may well be able

---

[217] Regulation 11(1)(a).
[218] Regulation 11(1)(b).
[219] Regulation 11(3).
[220] [1994] JBL 260, at p 268.

to reject them. Is the principal to blame for this consequence (which could arise in relation to breach of any of the implied terms under the Sale of Goods Act 1979)? Similar problems might arise where the principal has supplied information which constitutes an innocent misrepresentation entitling the third party to rescind. Again the principal may not be 'at fault', but his or her actions have prevented the execution of the transaction. Is this sufficient to mean that the principal is 'to blame', or does the agent have to establish that there has been at the least negligence on the part of the principal in order to maintain a claim for commission? It is submitted that since 'blame' and 'fault' are virtually interchangeable, the answer is that the principal will not be liable for commission where a non-negligent act has led to the failure of the contract with the third party. Thus where the cause is a totally innocent misdescription, or misrepresentation, the right to commission will be lost.

Where the right to commission has been lost under reg 11(1), any payment which has already been made must be refunded to the principal.[221]

The final obligations contained in Part III of the Regulations relates to the supply of information as to commission due and the right to inspect the principal's books. Like many of the other obligations in this Part of the regulations, they are non-derogable, and any agreement to deviate from them will be void.[222] These obligations are contained in reg 12. Regulation 12(1) requires the principal to supply the agent with a quarterly statement of commission due. The date on which this must be supplied is the same as the last date for payment of commission, ie the last day of the month following the quarter in which it became due. The statement must set out 'the main components used in calculating the commission'.[223] While principals may not regard this as a duty that they would as a matter of course owe to all agents, it is not one to which they could seriously object. The obligation in reg 12(2), however, is more controversial. This requires the principal to provide the agent, on demand, with the information necessary for the agent to check the amount of commission due. This information may, in particular, include 'an extract from the [principal's] books'. A principal might well regard this as information which is private, and not necessary to be disclosed in what is by definition a commercial relationship. It is important to note, however, that the agent has no right of *inspection* in the strict sense. The agent cannot demand access to the principal's accounts. The obligation is

---

[221] Regulation 11(2).
[222] Regulation 12(3).
[223] Regulation 12(1).

simply for the principal to extract the relevant information and provide it to the agent. What is provided is therefore largely in the hands of the principal. This factor, coupled with the lack of any specific remedy for a principal's failure to comply with either of the obligations contained in reg 13, may well mean that they are less onerous in practice than they appear on paper. The limited nature of the obligation is emphasised by reg 13(4) which specifically preserves any other enactment or rule of law which gives an agent a right to inspect the books of a principal. This ensures that the limited rights given by reg 13 are not regarded as superseding any more extensive right available under any other provision.

CHAPTER 4

PRINCIPAL AND THIRD PARTY

INTRODUCTION

In this chapter we are concerned with issues relating to the central purpose of the concept of agency. The main practical use of the concept is to allow a principal to come into a legal relationship with a third party. Here we are concerned with the precise incidents of the agency relationship and, in particular, the extent to which the principal and third party can sue or be sued by each other. Both contractual and tortious liabilities will need to be considered, though in the main we are concerned with contracts. Central to the discussion is the concept of authority. But whereas the emphasis in Chapter 3 was on the relationship between the principal and the agent, and the extent to which the agent could claim against the principal for commission, etc on the basis that actions were taken with authority, here we look at the issue of authority from the perspective of the third party. To what extent can the third party claim against the principal for acts by the agent which were, or appeared to be, done with authority?

Contractual liability will be discussed, and then liability in tort.

DISCLOSED AND UNDISCLOSED PRINCIPALS

Before discussing the rights and liabilities themselves, it is important to note that a principal may be disclosed, or undisclosed. Where the principal is disclosed, the third party knows from the start that they are dealing with an agent, and that there is another party in the background who will end up having legal rights against, and liabilities towards, the third party. The identity of this principal may be known, but this is not essential as long as the third party is aware that the agent is acting on behalf of another.[1] Where the principal is undisclosed, however, this means that the third party thinks the agent is acting on their own behalf. It is only after, for example, a contract has been made that the third

---

1   Note, however, that Bowstead identifies some cases where principals who are simply unnamed have been treated as undisclosed principals – *op cit*, p 316, citing, *inter alia, Addison v Gandessequi* (1812) 4 Taunt 574; *Teheran-Europe Co Ltd v ST Belton (Tractors) Ltd* [1968] 2 QB 545.

party may realise that there is a principal standing behind the agent, with whom the contract has in fact been made. Indeed, if a transaction goes through without problem it may be that the third party never realises at all that anyone other than the agent has been involved. Where problems arise, however, and there is the possibility of legal action, the existence of the undisclosed principal becomes very important.

The concept of the undisclosed principal clearly runs counter to the general contractual rule as to the necessity for privity of contract. The third party can find that they have rights against, and liabilities towards, a person with whom there was no intention to contract, and of whom the third party was in ignorance. For this reason, in the contractual sphere in particular, the situations where an undisclosed principal will be able to enforce a contract in place of the agent are subject to some restrictions, which are discussed below. There are no such restrictions, however, on the ability of the third party to sue the undisclosed principal, once that person's identity has been revealed.

The conceptual justification of allowing the undisclosed principal to sue a third party is unclear, and is generally regarded as anomalous, and something peculiar to English law. Some have argued it might be explained in terms of trust concepts,[2] but as Fridman has pointed out 'there seems little point in trying to explain what is really a common law relationship in terms which have an equitable flavour'.[3] Analogies with assignment of contracts have also been drawn.[4] The balance of opinion among both commentators and judges, however, is that the doctrine is best regarded as being based on practical and commercial convenience, despite the fact that it may produce injustice in some cases. As Lord Lindley pointed out in *Keighley, Maxsted & Co v Durant*,[5] in the great mass of commercial contracts the precise identity of the other contracting party is irrelevant. It would not contribute to the efficiency of such transactions to require an agent, on every occasion when acting for an undisclosed principal, to spell out that fact to the third party. Provided that some attempt is made to avoid the clearest injustices, then the doctrine can be regarded as a useful one.

The current law as regards undisclosed principals was recently summarised by the Privy Council in *Siu Yin Kwan v Eastern Insurance Co Ltd*[6] in the following way:

---

2   Eg Ames, *Undisclosed Principal – His Rights and Liabilities* (1909) 18 Yale LJ 443 discussed by Fridman, *op cit*, at pp 229–30.

3   *Op cit*, p 230.

4   Goodhart and Hamson (1932) 4 CLJ 320.

5   [1901] AC 240 at p 260.

6   [1994] 1 All ER 213 at p 220.

(1) An undisclosed principal may sue and be sued on a contract made by an agent on his behalf, acting within the scope of his actual authority. (2) In entering into the contract, the agent must intend to act on the principal's behalf. (3) The agent of an undisclosed principal may also sue and be sued on the contract. (4) Any defence which the third party may have against the agent is available against his principal. (5) The terms of the contract may, expressly or by implication, exclude the principal's right to sue, and his liability to be sued. The contract itself or the circumstances surrounding the contract, may show that the agent is the true and only principal.

We need to concentrate on the rules that operate under (5), developed in order to avoid the potential injustices referred to above. The avoidance of such injustices is the principal reason for the various restrictions placed on an undisclosed principal who wishes to enforce a contract. The first restriction is that the existence of an undisclosed principal must not be inconsistent with the terms of the contract. In *Humble v Hunter*,[7] a charterparty stated that it was between 'CJ Humble, Esq, owner of the good ship or vessel called the "Ann"' and the defendants. CJ Humble's mother, Grace, tried to bring evidence that her son, in making the charterparty, was acting as agent for her. It was held that the description of the son as 'owner' of the vessel was inconsistent with his being an agent for somebody else.[8] The attempt by Grace to take over the contract as an undisclosed principal therefore failed. This decision may be contrasted with that in *Fred Drughorn Ltd v Rederiaktiebolaget Transatlantic*.[9] Here, one of the parties to a charterparty, L, was described as the 'charterer'. A dispute on the charter arose, but L died before the trial came on. The Swedish company of which L was the manager tried to replace him in the action, claiming that he had been acting as their agent. The House of Lords affirmed the view of the trial judge and Court of Appeal that this was permissible. As Viscount Haldane commented:[10]

> The term "charterer" is a very different term from the term "owner" or the term "proprietor". A charterer may be and *prima facie* is merely entering into a contract. A charterparty is not a lease ... and although rights of ownership or rights akin to ownership may be given under it *prima facie* it is a contract for the hiring or use of the vessel. Under these circumstances it is in accordance with ordinary business common-sense and custom that charterers should be able to contract as agents for undisclosed principals who may come in and take the benefit of the charterparty.

---

7 (1848) 12 QB 310.
8 Following *Lucas v De La Cour* (1813) 1 M&S 249.
9 [1919] AC 203.
10 *Ibid*, at p 207.

In other words, the particular terminology used in the contract must be considered, to see if it is inconsistent with agency. 'Charterer' simply denotes a person's particular role in a contract, and is not inconsistent with the person being an agent; 'owner' or 'proprietor', however, connotes property rights, and it is inconsistent that a person who is the 'owner' of property should act as agent for someone else in a contract relating to it. This decision illustrates the limitations of the rule applied in *Humble v Hunter*. Nevertheless, care needs to be taken in respect of the use of terminology in a contract where an apparent contracting party is in fact acting for an undisclosed principal.

The second limitation relates to personal considerations, which may be relevant to certain types of contract. If the character of the other contracting party is an important consideration to the third party, an undisclosed principal may be prevented from stepping into the agent's shoes. An example of this is *Collins v Associated Greyhound Racecourses*.[11] Two people made an application to underwrite a share issue. They were in fact acting as agents for C, an undisclosed principal. C later sought to rescind the contract for the purchase of the shares on the basis of a misrepresentation in the prospectus. The Court of Appeal, however, refused to allow him to take over this contract. An underwriting contract was one where the character of the underwriter was important. As Lord Hanworth put it:[12] 'It was necessary for the company to form an opinion as to whether or not they should take objection within a limited time to the sub-underwriters who were being put forward as being responsible persons.'

This was important because if the underwriters failed to fulfill their commitment to take up shares unplaced elsewhere, this could place the company in severe financial difficulties. There was therefore significant personal element in the contract, which meant that those who purported to make the agreement should in fact be the contracting parties.

The personal considerations need not relate to the financial probity of the other party (as in *Collins*). In *Said v Butt*,[13] for example, the undisclosed principal had asked the agent to obtain a theatre ticket for the first night of a play. This was done because the principal knew that the manager of the theatre, because of previous disputes, would refuse to supply him with a ticket, and had indeed done so when he had applied in person. On arriving at the theatre he was refused admission by the manager. McCardie J held that the theatre was entitled to take this action:[14]

---

[11] [1930] Ch 1.
[12] *Ibid*, at p 32.
[13] [1920] 3 KB 497.
[14] *Ibid*, at p 503.

I hold that by the mere device of utilising the name and services of Mr Pollock [the "agent"], the plaintiff could not constitute himself a contractor with the Palace Theatre against their knowledge, and contrary to their express refusal. He is disabled from asserting that he was the undisclosed principal of Mr Pollock.

This quotation seems to suggest that mere knowledge of the fact that the third party would not wish to contract with the principal is enough to exclude the operation of the doctrine of the undisclosed principal. This is contradicted, however, by *Dyster v Randall*.[15] The plaintiff wished to buy a piece of land owned by the defendants. He knew that they would not deal with him, because he had been dismissed from a company which the defendants had helped to promote in circumstances which led them to distrust him. He therefore acted through C. In an action for specific performance it was held that the plaintiff was entitled, as an undisclosed principal, to bring the action. The reason was that the personality of the purchaser was not a material ingredient in this contract. This can only be reconciled with *Said v Butt* on the basis that the decision in that case was not based on the plaintiff's knowledge of the theatre's attitude towards him, but because, at least in relation to a 'first night', the theatre's management is entitled to exercise control over who is in the audience. The issue then becomes one of personal considerations, and the type of contract concerned, rather than knowledge. The decision in *Collins* was based primarily on the type of contract; that in *Said v Butt* on a combination of the type of contract and the personalities involved.

The area of personal contracts and undisclosed principals was recently reconsidered by the Privy Council in *Siu Yin Kwan v Eastern Insurance Co Ltd*.[16] It was held that a contract of indemnity insurance is not of itself a 'personal' contract of a type whereby an undisclosed principal is prevented from taking it over from an agent.[17]

The undisclosed principal may also be excluded where the problem is not that the third party is unwilling to contract with the principal, but that they wish to contract exclusively with the agent. *Greer v Downs Supply Co*[18] provides an example. The contract was one of sale of goods, to which personal considerations would usually be irrelevant. The purchaser, however, was owed money by the 'agent' who sold the goods to him. The existence of this debt was sufficient to mean that the purchaser was not liable to an 'undisclosed principal' who tried to sue

---

15 [1926] 1 Ch 932.
16 [1994] 1 All ER 213.
17 Following *Browning v Provincial Insurance Co of Canada* (1873) LR 5 PC 263.
18 [1927] 2 KB 28.

on the contract. In this context, the personal considerations were sufficient to prevent the doctrine operating.

With the distinctions between, and the possible implications of, the concepts of the disclosed and undisclosed principal in mind, we can now consider the principal's rights and liabilities towards the third party.

CONTRACTUAL LIABILITY

We are concerned here with the situation where the agent negotiates a contract with the third party. Provided that the contract is, or can be regarded as having been, made within the agent's authority, the principal will be bound. There are three types of authority to be considered – express, implied and ostensible.

Express authority

This needs little discussion here. We have already considered this topic in the context of the relationship between principal and agent.[19] As far as this type of authority is concerned the liability of the principal will be co-terminous with it. In other words, if the agent has acted within express authority in negotiating a contract with the third party, then the principal will be bound to it. It is irrelevant for these purposes whether the third party is aware of the precise terms of the express authority.

Whether the third party is bound will depend on whether the principal is disclosed or undisclosed. If disclosed, then the third party will definitely be bound; if undisclosed, the principal's ability to enforce against the third party will depend on the rules relating to undisclosed principals, discussed above.

Ostensible authority

This type of authority is sometimes referred to as 'apparent'. It also encompasses the concept of 'agency by estoppel', under which P's words or actions may lead others to believe that A is P's agent, when in fact this is not the case. The concept can thus, in some circumstances, create an agency relationship, at least as far as principal and third party are concerned.[20] It does not, however, affect the relationship between an existing principal and agent (eg in terms of legitimising an agent's

---

[19] Chapter 3, p 42.
[20] See for example, *Freeman & Lockyer v Buckhurst Park Properties (Mangal) Ltd* [1964] 2 QB 480, discussed further below, p 101.

breach of the duty to follow instructions),[21] nor will it create a relationship of principal and agent between two persons who have no such prior relationship.

What are the requirements for this type of authority? In *Rama Corporation Ltd v Proved Tin and General Investments Ltd*,[22] Slade J said that ostensible authority , being a kind of estoppel, required: '(i) a representation, (ii) a reliance on the representation, and (iii) an alteration of your position resulting from such reliance'.[23] These requirements will be considered in turn.

Representation

The precise nature of the representation required was expanded on by Diplock LJ in *Freeman & Lockyer v Buckhurst Park Properties (Mangal) Ltd*[24] in the following passage:[25]

> "ostensible" authority, on the other hand, is a legal relationship between the principal and the contractor created by a representation, *made by the principal to the contractor*, intended to be and in fact acted upon by the contractor, that the agent has authority to enter on behalf of the principal into a contract of a kind within the scope of the "apparent" authority so as to render the principal liable to perform any obligations imposed upon him by such a contract. (emphasis added)

Moreover, the agent 'must not purport to make the agreement as principal himself'.[26] There is no room in this area for the undisclosed principal. Indeed, such an idea would be logically inconsistent with a requirement of a representation from the principal. It is also implicit in the definitions noted above that the representation should come from the principal rather than the agent. This point was confirmed by the House of Lords in *Armagas v Mundogas*.[27]

Magelssen was the vice-president (transportation) and chartering manager of Mundogas, who were trying to sell a particular ship. Johannsen, a partner in a firm of shipbrokers, was helping to arrange the sale. Armagas was interested in purchasing the vessel, but only if at the same time Mundogas would charter it back for three years. Magelssen had no authority, or prospect of obtaining authority, for such a deal.

---

21 See Chapter 3, p 47.
22 [1952] 2 QB 147.
23 *Ibid*, at pp 149–150.
24 [1964] 2 QB 480.
25 *Ibid*, at p 503.
26 *Ibid*.
27 [1986] 2 All ER 385.

Nevertheless, he and Johannsen conspired to deceive Armagas into thinking that such authority had been specifically given by Mundogas, and documents for the sale and charter back were signed. Magelssen and Johannsen planned to make a secret profit out of this transaction. Unfortunately for them, market rates for charters moved in such a way as to make their plan incapable of fulfilment, and their deceit came to light. Armagas sued Mundogas on the basis of the three-year charter. The House of Lords upheld the view of the Court of Appeal that Magelssen's position as vice-president (transportation) and chartering manager would not have been taken as giving him ostensible authority to enter into such an transaction. Moreover, the representations of specific authority could not bind Mundogas, since they came from Magelssen and Johannsen who were only agents. For a representation to give rise to ostensible authority it must emanate from the principal. As Lord Keith put it '[N]o representation by Mr Magelssen can help Armagas. It must be in a position to found on some relevant representation by the responsible management of Mundogas as to Mr Magelssen's authority'.[28]

Although the courts talk in terms of 'representations' they do not in this context necessarily mean a 'statement of existing fact'. The principal's behaviour can at times be treated as a representation. Thus in *Summers v Solomon*[29] the defendant owned a jewellers shop, and employed a manager to run it. The defendant regularly paid for jewellery that the manager ordered from the plaintiff. The manager left his employment, ordered jewellery from the plaintiff in the defendant's name, and absconded with it. The plaintiff sued the defendant for the cost of the jewellery, and succeeded. The defendant's previous conduct caused the plaintiff to believe that the manager had authority to pledge his credit. This behaviour amounted to a sufficient representation to bring ostensible authority into play. Indeed, it seems that the only way in which the defendant could have avoided the effects of the doctrine would have been to inform the plaintiff that the manager's agency had come to an end.

There was, if anything, even less of a representation in *Lloyd v Grace, Smith & Co*.[30] Mrs Lloyd owned two cottages and a sum of money secured on a mortgage. Dissatisfied with the return she was getting, she called at the defendants' office. She saw a Mr Sandles, whom she took to be a partner, though in fact he was only the managing clerk. Sandles had authority, however, to conduct conveyancing business without supervision. Acting in the name of the firm, he tricked Mrs Lloyd into

---

28 *Ibid*, at p 390.
29 (1857) E&B 879.
30 [1912] AC 716.

conveying her property to him, and then disposed of it for his own benefit. It was held by the House of Lords that the firm was responsible for Sandle's conduct. By allowing him to deal with conveyancing, the firm had represented that he had authority to get clients to agree to transfers of their property.

Thus, there is no need for a statement, or even any specific act or omission. Merely putting the agent into a position where the third party would think that authority had been given is sufficient. This approach was perhaps taken to its extreme in *Freeman & Lockyer v Buckhurst Park Properties (Mangal) Ltd*.[31] A man called Kapoor, a property developer, had a plan to buy and sell a large estate. He formed a company for this purpose, together with two other people, who put in capital. Kapoor was never given the position of managing director of the company, but to the knowledge of the others acted as such in making contracts for the company. The plaintiffs were architects who did work on the estate. The planned resale of the property never took place, and the plaintiffs sued the company. By this time Kapoor had disappeared. An attempt was made to argue that Kapoor had never been authorised to act on behalf of the company. This was rejected by the Court of Appeal. The other two members of the company, by not intervening when they knew that Kapoor was acting as if managing director, had given him ostensible authority to act on behalf of the company. As far as the requirement of a 'representation' was concerned, Diplock LJ pointed out that:

> The representation which creates "apparent" authority may take a variety of forms, of which the commonest is representation by conduct, that is, by permitting the agent to act in some way in the conduct of the principal's business with other persons.[32]

The facts of *Freeman* confirm that this representation by conduct can include representation by omission. Failing to intervene when you know that the 'agent' is acting in a particular way may be deemed to constitute a representation to the world that the actions are authorised. All this shows that the requirement of a representation is a very flexible one, which has received a very broad interpretation by the courts.

Reliance

The second of Slade J's requirements was that there must be reliance on the representation. This means that the third party will not be able plead reliance on the agent's ostensible authority if:

---

31 [1964] 2 QB 480.
32 *Ibid*, at p 503.

- the third party did not know of the relevant conduct by the principal;
- the third party did not actually believe that the agent had authority; or
- the third party ought to have known that the agent's authority had been limited.

The first two limitations are straightforward questions of fact. The third, raising the concept of constructive notice, is more complex. In what circumstances will it be considered that the third party, who does not know of the limitations of the agent's authority, *ought*, nevertheless, to have known? An example of the application of this requirement is found in *Overbrooke Estates Ltd v Glencombe Properties*.[33] The plaintiffs put a house up for sale by auction. The auctioneers told the defendant that the local authorities had no plans for the property, and were not interested in it for compulsory purchase. The defendant bought the house at auction. The general conditions of sale stated that:

> The vendors do not make or give and neither the auctioneers nor any person in the employment of the auctioneers has any authority to make or give any representation or warranty in relation to these properties.

After the auction the defendant discovered from the local authority that the property might be destined for slum clearance. As a result, the defendant tried to withdraw from the contract. The plaintiff sued for specific performance. The defendant relied on the statements made by the auctioneers, as agents for the plaintiffs. Brightman J, however, held for the plaintiffs. He commented:

> It seems to me that it must be open to a principal to draw the attention of the public to the limits which he places on the authority of his agent, and that this must be so whether the agent is a person who has, or has not, any ostensible authority. If an agent has *prima facie* some ostensible authority, that authority is inevitably diminished to the extent of the publicised limits that are placed upon it.

Whether or not the defendants in fact knew of the restrictions contained in the conditions of sale, they ought to have done, and this prevented their reliance on any ostensible authority in relation to the statements concerning local authority interest in the property.

There must be alteration of position

This means that the third party must have suffered some detriment, or at least taken some action, on the basis of the ostensible authority. It seems,

---

[33] [1974] 3 All ER 511.

however, that merely entering into a contract on the basis of it will be sufficient, so in practice this point seems to add little to the previous one, that the third party must rely on the representation. In any case, it is difficult to imagine circumstances giving rise to an action by a third party, which did not involve some change of position.

Note that ostensible authority does not of itself allow a principal to enforce a contract against a third party. The concept exists primarily to protect the third party, and, as has been noted above, it does not create an agency relationship between the principal and the agent. There is no reason, therefore, why it should create any rights for the principal.

Implied authority

It is in relation to this type of authority that confusion is most likely to arise. This is because of the failure of the courts to distinguish between authority implied as between principal and agent, and authority implied for the purposes of entitling the third party to sue. The difference becomes important where there is an express limitation on the agent's authority. The agent who acts contrary to this express restriction will not be able to claim that their actions were impliedly authorised for the purpose of recovering commission, etc. On the contrary, the agent is likely to be in breach of contract *vis-à-vis* the principal, and certainly will be in breach of the obligation to obey instructions.[34] On the other hand, the third party who is unaware of the express restriction will be entitled to rely on the agent's implied authority, and take action against the principal on this basis.

A case which, while not without some difficulty, shows these principles in operation is *Watteau v Fenwick*.[35] A man called Humble had carried on business at a beerhouse called the Victoria Hotel, Stockton-on-Tees, for a number of years. At some point he had sold the business to Fenwick & Co, who were brewers, but he had remained as manager, the licence for the premises was in his name, and his name was painted over the door. Under his agreement with Fenwick & Co, Humble had no authority to buy any goods for the business except bottled ales and mineral waters. For some years Watteau supplied goods to Humble on credit. As far as Watteau was concerned, he was dealing with Humble as principal, and had no knowledge that Humble was not the owner of the business. Humble, however, failed to pay for certain cigars and bovril, and Watteau then discovered that Fenwick & Co were the true owners

---

[34] See Chapter 2, p 47.
[35] [1893] 1 QB 346.

of the hotel. He sued them for the value of the goods supplied. The county court judge allowed the claim, and the High Court upheld that decision.

Humble had clearly acted outside his actual authority. On what basis, then, were Fenwick & Co liable for this contract? Wills J, giving the judgment of the court, recognised the argument that a principal should be liable only where there has been a holding out of authority, but rejected it. If this were the law then:[36] 'In every case of undisclosed principal ... the secret limitation of authority would prevail and defeat the action of the person dealing with the agent and then discovering that he was an agent and had a principal'. He thought that this could not be the case, because it was clearly established in partnership law that no limitation of authority as between dormant and active partner will protect the dormant partner as to things within the ordinary authority of a partner. Since the law of partnership is on this issue simply a branch of the general law of agency, the same approach should apply in situations other than partnership. The true principle was that apparently stated during argument, by Lord Coleridge:[37] 'That the principal is liable for all the acts of the agent which are within the authority usually confided to an agent of that character, notwithstanding limitations, as between the principal and the agent, put upon that authority'.

What is needed, then, for implied authority as in *Watteau v Fenwick* is that there should be an existing agency relationship,[38] and that the agency should be of such a character that it is possible to identify the 'usual' powers that such an agent will have. The extent of these powers is a question of fact. Once identified, they will constitute the usual authority of the agent. A contrast can be drawn with the similar case of *Daun v Simmins*.[39] This again concerned a public house, but on this occasion one which the third party was aware was 'tied' to a particular brewer. It was held that the manager of such a public house would not usually have authority to buy spirits other than from persons specified by the brewer. As a result there was no implied authority on which the third party could rely.

This type of implied authority is that which 'usually' attaches to the particular type of work being done by the agent, and can therefore be designated 'usual' authority. A recent case which, it may be argued, shows this type of authority in operation (though it is not the way in which the court concerned analysed the relationship) is *City Trust v*

---

36 *Ibid*, at p 349.

37 *Ibid*, at p 348.

38 Unlike ostensible authority, which can operate where no agency has existed, or where it has been terminated.

39 (1879) 41 LT 783.

Levy.[40] Here the issue was the power of an assistant solicitor to give an undertaking which was binding on his firm, in relation to the debts of a client. It was held that a solicitor would usually have such a power, provided there was a relevant fund under the control of the firm, which 'must come into their hands in the course of some ulterior transaction which is itself the sort of work which solicitors undertake'.[41]

Despite the fact that the Court of Appeal preferred to discuss the case in terms of ostensible or apparent authority, it is submitted that the quotation above, and others like it, indicate that the Court was in effect identifying a type of usual authority, attaching to the position of assistant solicitor.[42]

A further type of implied authority can arise from the *place* of work, rather than the *type* of work which is being done. If it is the custom that agents working in a particular place of trade have particular types of authority, the third party will be entitled to rely on it, in the absence of any specific indication that this authority has been withdrawn by the principal. As Parke B put it in *Bayliffe v Butterworth*:[43]

[I]f there is, at a particular place, an established usage in the manner of dealing and making contracts, a person who is employed to deal or make a contract there has an implied authority to act in the usual way.[44]

In *Scott v Godfrey*,[45] for example, a custom of the London Stock Exchange which permitted stockbrokers to buy shares for several principals from a single seller was held to bind each principal to the seller. This was so even though at the time of the purchase the shares were not allocated as between the different principals. Similarly a custom of the Liverpool wool market whereby a broker may buy either in their own name, or that of the principal, was upheld in *Cropper v Crook*,[46] even though the principal was unaware of the custom.

A particular characteristic of usual authority which potentially arises from the fact that it is not dependent on a representation from the principal, is that it may be available in relation to an agent who is working for an undisclosed principal. This was the situation in *Watteau v*

---

40 [1988] 3 All ER 418.
41 *Ibid*, at pp 427–8, *per* Staughton LJ.
42 Stone, RTH, 'Usual and ostensible authority – one concept or two?' [1993] JB 325. Cf *First Energy (UK) Ltd v Hungarian International Bank Ltd* [1993] 2 Lloyd's Rep 194, discussed below at p 106.
43 (1847) 1 Ex. 425.
44 *Ibid*, at p 428.
45 [1901] 2 KB 726.
46 (1868) LR 3 CP 194.

Fenwick[47] itself. It is an aspect of the case which has been the subject of adverse comment from judges and commentators. On more than one occasion a Canadian court has refused to follow it.[48] In this country, Bingham J in *Rhodian River Shipping Co SA v Halla Maritime Corporation*[49] came close to rejecting it. And Bowstead only includes it as a principle with hesitation.[50]

RELATIONSHIP BETWEEN USUAL AND OSTENSIBLE AUTHORITY

The courts have not always distinguished very carefully between ostensible and usual authority. This is shown by the decision in *City Trust v Levy*, discussed above.[51] The confusion arises from the fact that in many cases the principal may be said to have given the agent ostensible authority to perform all the usual transactions of an agent of a particular type. This follows from the decision in *Freeman Lockyer v Buckhurst*, where simply allowing a person to act in a particular capacity was held to be a representation of their authority to do so. Once this is accepted, the need for a separate category of 'usual authority' becomes much reduced. The decision in *Watteau v Fenwick*, however, stands as authority for the proposition that usual authority can arise in respect of the agent of an undisclosed principal. If that is possible, then there must be situations where usual authority can have an independent existence. If the third party is unaware, at the time of the contract, of the *existence* of the principal, it cannot be said that the third party has been misled by any representation from the principal. Although, as we have seen, this aspect of *Watteau v Fenwick* has been much criticised, and has been rejected by courts in other jurisdictions, it has never been overruled by an English court. A recent decision of the Court of Appeal, however, has once again illustrated the close link between usual and ostensible authority, and the fact that in some cases the requirement of a representation of authority from the principal can become so watered down as to be nearly non-existent. The case is *First Energy (UK) Ltd v Hungarian International Bank Ltd*.[52]

---

47   [1893] 1 QB 346; above p 103.
48   *McLaughlin v Gentles* (1919) 51 DLR 383; *Massey Harris v Bond* [1930] 2 DLR 57; *Sign-O-Lite Plastics Ltd v Metropolitan Life Assurance Co* [1990] 73 DLR (4th) 541.
49   [1984] 1 Lloyd's Rep 373.
50   *Op cit*, pp 317–20.
51   See p 104.
52   [1993] 2 Lloyd's LR 194.

The agent in this case was J, who was the defendant's senior manager in charge of their Manchester office. He was closely involved with lengthy negotiations with the plaintiffs in connection with the establishment of their business, which involved the installation of heating systems in commercial buildings. The plaintiffs wished to provide credit facilities to customers, so that payment for the heating installation could be spread over a number of years. They sought assistance from the defendants in providing such facilities. The defendants were initially favourably disposed towards the plaintiffs, and a hire-purchase facility was arranged in respect of the first installation undertaken by them. Further installation contracts were then obtained by the plaintiffs, and they sought additional credit arrangements, totalling just over £600,000. J wrote a letter to the plaintiffs which carried the implication that approval had been given for the provision of funds to support these arrangements. In fact no such approval had been given, but the plaintiffs relied on J's letter and proceeded accordingly. Shortly afterwards, the senior management of the defendants decided they did not wish to carry on with any arrangements with the plaintiffs, and purported to withdraw from any commitment to finance the £600,000 worth of business.

The plaintiffs sued on the basis that they had accepted an offer to provide these credit facilities, made by J as agent for the defendants. It was common ground that J had no actual authority to sanction the provision of a credit facility, since this had been made clear by J at an early stage of the negotiations. The case was therefore argued on the basis of an ostensible authority to communicate the fact that such a provision had been approved by the defendants. The problem for the plaintiffs was that, since all dealings were with J, in what sense could the defendants be said to have made a representation of his authority? The defendants relied on *Armagas Ltd v Mundogas SA*,[53] where, as we have seen, the House of Lords ruled that an agent cannot be 'self-authorising' for the purpose of ostensible authority; there must be some representation from the principal. The trial judge nevertheless found in favour of the plaintiffs, and the defendants appealed.

Steyn LJ started his discussion of this issue by noting that 'usual authority' can have two meanings:[54]

> First, it sometimes means that the agent had implied actual authority to perform acts necessarily incidental to the performance of the agency. Secondly, it sometimes means that the principal's conduct in clothing the agent with the trappings of authority was such as to

---

[53] [1986] 1 AC 717, discussed above at p 99.
[54] [1993] 2 Lloyd's LR 194 at p 201.

induce a third party to rely on the existence of the agency. The issue in the present case is one of usual authority in the second sense.

Having introduced the concept of 'usual authority', however, Steyn LJ goes on to discuss the case purely in terms of ostensible authority. His analysis of the relationships between the parties led him to the conclusion that, although J did not have ostensible authority to enter into the credit transaction on behalf of the defendants, he did have ostensible authority to communicate to the plaintiffs that such a transaction had been approved. A serious difficulty in the way of this conclusion was the speech of Lord Keith in *Armagas v Mundogas*, where he quoted with approval the comments of Robert Goff LJ in the Court of Appeal, who described as 'extraordinary' the attempt which had been made in that case to draw a distinction between:

(1) a case where an agent having no ostensible authority to enter into the relevant contract, wrongly asserts that he is invested with actual authority to do so, in which event the principal is not bound; and (2) a case where an agent, having no ostensible authority, wrongly asserts after negotiations that he has gone back to his principal and obtained actual authority, in which event the principal is bound. As a matter of common sense, this is most unlikely to be the law.[55]

Lord Keith, in agreeing with this conclusion, commented:

It must be a most unusual and peculiar case where an agent who is known to have no general authority to enter into transactions of a certain type can by reason of circumstances created by the principal be believed to have specific authority to enter into a particular transaction of that type.[56]

This might well have been thought to be fatal to the argument being put forward by the plaintiffs. Steyn LJ noted, however, that Lord Keith did not entirely rule out the possibility of an agent being authorised to communicate approval even where they have no authority to enter into the transaction itself: it is simply categorised as a rare occurrence. Steyn LJ also drew support from the obiter comments of Browne-Wilkinson LJ, in *Egyptian International Foreign Trade Co v Soplex Wholesale Supplies Ltd*.[57] He suggested that although an agent who had no authority to enter into a transaction, or to make representations as to the transaction, clearly could not 'hold himself out as having authority to enter into the transaction so as to effect [sic] the principal's position',[58] the position might be different if the agent does have authority to make

---

55 [1986] 1 AC 717, at pp 730–1.
56 *Ibid*, at p 779.
57 [1985] 2 Lloyd's Rep 36.
58 *Ibid*, at p 43.

representations. In such a situation, Browne-Wilkinson LJ said: 'I am inclined to think an agent with authority to make representations can make a representation that he has authority to enter into a transaction.'

It should be noted that this comment was made prior to the House of Lords decision in *Armagas v Mundogas*. Nevertheless, Steyn LJ thought it was helpful to the plaintiffs, and indicated that the approach which should be adopted in such cases was similar to that taken in the company law cases on 'indoor management', best exemplified by *Royal British Bank v Turquand*,[59] under which a third party dealing with a company's agent was entitled to assume that the company's internal rules had been complied with. The specific examples then used are of a company secretary, and a managing director, where it would not be expected that a person dealing with them would need to insist that verification directly from the Board would be needed of any indication from them that a particular transaction had received Board approval. This is true. But it is submitted that an unacknowledged shift has been made from the concept of ostensible authority to that of usual authority. Company secretaries and managing directors are clearly people who have usual authority attaching to them, simply from the position they hold within the company. There is, thus, no need for any specific 'holding-out' of such a person's authority. In the present case, however, J was not a company secretary or managing director. He was a senior manager, but did not hold a position in relation to which it would be possible to identify the 'usual' incidents. His only authority, beyond his actual authority, therefore, had to be 'ostensible'. This required a 'holding-out' by his employers: but no such 'holding-out' had been identified, and it is submitted that the decision ought therefore to have gone against the plaintiffs in this case.

The other members of the Court of Appeal[60] likewise drew a distinction between authority to enter into a transaction, and authority to communicate approval for a transaction, and on this basis found in favour of the plaintiffs. The distinction being drawn, however, is in the type of situation that occurred in this case, a distinction without a difference. A manager whose authority to enter into a transaction has been specifically limited by their principal, can apparently avoid this restriction simply by saying 'The Board has given its approval'. If this is all that is required, why not simply say that the manager has authority to enter into the transaction itself, since that is the effective result of the

---

[59] (1855) E&B 248. See also, Stone, 'Usual and ostensible authority' [1993] JBL 325, at p 335

[60] Nourse and Evans LJJ.

analysis? Given that this seems to have been specifically rejected by the House of Lords in *Armagas v Mundogas* it is difficult to accept that *First Energy v HIB* was correctly decided.[61]

Another Court of Appeal decision, handed down shortly before *First Energy v HIB*, is much easier to reconcile with earlier authority, though it again deals in part with the relationship between usual and ostensible authority. This is *Gurtner v Beaton*.[62] The case resulted from an air crash. The agency point at issue was whether Beaton, who had arranged the flight did so as agent for a company called Cleanacres Ltd. B had been employed by the firm part-time as 'aviation manager'. His duties were to provide tuition in flying and to supervise maintenance of the company's aircraft. At the same time B was allowed by the company to carry out various other activities, under the name 'Cleanacres Aviation'. This included the provision of tuition, using Cleanacres Ltd's aircraft. In fact, however, B also engaged in 'air-taxi' work, ie carrying passengers for reward. This was unlawful, because B did not have an 'air operator's certificate' (AOC) issued by the Civil Aviation Authority. Nor did Cleanacres Ltd. The crash that led to the legal action arose out of a such an unlawful contract. The issue for decision was whether B had either implied actual authority, or ostensible authority, to carry out air-taxi work. The trial judge held that B had authority on both bases, and that Cleanacres Ltd were therefore liable as 'carriers' of the passengers on the ill-fated flight.

The Court of Appeal considered first the issue of implied actual authority. Here they took the view that there was no such authority. Nothing from the evidence showed that Cleanacres Ltd were aware of the unlawful air-taxi work 'or would have permitted it, or were willing to tolerate it provided that it was concealed by pretences'.[63] On the contrary, the evidence suggested that if B had asked permission to do such work it would have been refused, and that B knew this.

Turning, however, to ostensible authority (referred to in the judgment as 'apparent authority'), the Court of Appeal agreed with the trial judge. The reason for this was that the extension from the work which B had implied actual authority to carry out, ie carrying third parties where the pilot was under instruction, to work which was not actually authorised, ie carrying third parties simply for reward, was one the significance of which would be not be apparent to an actual or potential customer. As far as such a person was concerned, B was acting as the Aviation Manager of Cleanacres Ltd, operating as Cleanacres

---

61 *Cf* Reynolds, [1994] JBL 144, at p 146.
62 [1993] 2 Lloyd's LR 369.
63 *Ibid*, at p 376.

Aviation, and in this context there was nothing to suggest that he did not have authority to carry out air-taxi work, and the proper legal permissions (ie an AOC) to do this.

In coming to this conclusion, Neill J made reference to the analysis of ostensible authority by Diplock LJ in *Freeman & Lockyer v Buckhurst Park Properties (Mangal) Ltd.*[64] In particular, he noted Diplock LJ's comment that the representation required for ostensible authority may often come from the principal's conduct in allowing the agent to act in particular ways, and that:[65]

> By so doing the principal represents to anyone who becomes aware that the agent is so acting that the agent has authority to enter on behalf of the principal into contracts with other persons of the kind which an agent so acting in the conduct of the principal's business has *usually* "actual" authority to enter into (emphasis added).

Neill LJ commented that it would be wrong to concentrate on the word 'usually' in this passage, so that an 'aviation manager' could not 'be regarded as "usually" having authority to make a contract for air taxi work when the aviation business of which he is manager does not include such work'.[66]

This must be right, and it highlights the difference between 'usual' and 'ostensible' authority. 'Usual authority' will always be limited to the usual incidents of being a person holding a particular position, such as 'aviation manager'. Just because a person's job is labelled in a particular way, however, does not mean that they cannot have a wider authority as far as third parties are concerned, based on 'ostensible authority'. Provided that the words or actions of the principal are sufficient to indicate such wider authority, then the third party is justified in relying on it, even if it goes beyond what would normally be expected of an agent holding that position. The judgment of the Court of Appeal in this case, delivered by Neill LJ, contains a clear analysis of the issues in this area, and has with justification been characterised by one commentator as 'an excellent decision'.[67]

TORTIOUS LIABILITY

To what extent is the principal liable to a third party for tortious acts of the agent? The principles in this area bear a close relationship to the

---

[64] [1964] 2 QB 480. See above, p 101.

[65] *Ibid*, at p 503.

[66] [1993] 2 Lloyd's LR 369, at p 379.

[67] Reynolds [1994] JBL 144.

principles of vicarious liability which operate in relation to employers and employees.[68] Indeed, in the situation where an agent is also an employee there is little need to investigate the situation from the point of view of agency. The principal/employer will be liable for all the tortious actions of the agent/employee performed in the 'course of employment'. The principles applying in this area are fully discussed in any standard tort text,[69] and it is not proposed to deal with them in any detail here. The identification of the scope of the concept of 'course of employment' involves considering whether the employee's actions formed part of their duties. It should be noted, however, that the fact that the employee deliberately carries out a duty in a way that contravenes an express instruction from the employer does not in itself prevent vicarious liability from operating.[70]

Turning to the position in relation to the agent *stricto sensu*, the first point to note is that in some cases the principal may be directly, rather than vicariously, liable for the acts of the agent.[71] If, for example, the principal tells the agent to sell certain goods that in fact belong to a third party (though the agent thinks they belong to the principal), the principal will be liable for conversion. The agent will have acted simply as a tool for carrying out the principal's tortious enterprise. In other words, where the agent acts on express instructions to carry out an action which is tortious, the principal will be liable in his own right. The agent may also be liable, as where the instruction is to carry out an assault. Here the agent is fully aware of the tortious nature of the task, and will be jointly liable with the principal. This approach can be applied to a slightly more likely circumstance by considering the position where the agent is told to make a false statement in order to induce a contract. Both principal and agent may be liable for the tort of deceit.[72] In the same way, the principal will also be liable for any unauthorised acts that are subsequently ratified. Thus an unauthorised purchase of goods by an agent from a third party who has no right to sell will amount to conversion by the agent: the principle who then ratifies the unauthorised purchase will also be liable.[73] The requirements for ratification are discussed in Chapter 2.[74]

---

68 Eg *Winfield and Jolowicz on Tort* (14th edn), Ch 21.

69 *Ibid.*

70 See eg *Limpus v London General Omnibus Co* (1862) 1 H&C 526; *Rose v Plenty* [1976] 1 WLR 141.

71 See Bowstead, Article 97(2)(a), and p 291.

72 *Cf Armstrong v Strain* [1952] 1 KB 232.

73 *Hilberry v Hatton* (1864) 2 H&C 822.

74 Page 25.

Where the agent acts other than on specific instructions, and in the absence of subsequent ratification, the issue arises as to whether the principal is nevertheless vicariously liable. It seems that if the actions of the agent fall outside any actual, implied or ostensible authority, the principal will not be so liable. This was the view of the Court of Appeal and House of Lords in *Armagas Ltd v Mundogas SA*.[75] The facts of this case have been given above.[76] Both the appeal courts took the view that the fact that the statements were made without authority (actual or ostensible) protected the principal from being vicariously liable for them. The case was concerned with fraudulent misrepresentations, and the *dicta* on this topic are particularly linked to this type of tort. It is submitted, however, that there is no reason not to apply the same approach in other areas, at least where the agent is not also an employee. In *Armagas Ltd v Mundogas SA* the maker of the statement was also an employee, and it was held that the concepts of actual and ostensible authority were co-terminous with that of 'course of employment' as far as the making of statements is concerned. That is, the employee who makes statements without any authority will not be regarded as acting in the course of employment. In other areas, however, it may be that the concept of 'course of employment' is wider than that of 'authority'. In *Navarro v Moregrand Ltd*[77] Denning LJ expressed the view that an employer is liable for acts done 'in the course of employment', whether or not they are also done with 'authority': 'The presence of actual or ostensible authority is decisive to show that his conduct is within the course of his employment, but the absence of it is not decisive the other way.'[78]

The House of Lords in *Armagas Ltd v Mundogas SA*, while disagreeing with this approach insofar as it might apply to statements, did not overrule it more generally. It may therefore be taken still to represent the law on this issue, where the agent is also an employee. Where that is not the case, however, there seems no reason to depart from the approach that the extent of the principal's vicarious liability for the acts of a non-employee agent is bounded by the concepts of actual and ostensible authority.

---

[75] [1985] 1 Lloyd's Rep 1; affirmed by the House of Lords at [1986] 2 All ER 385.

[76] Page 99.

[77] [1951] 2 TLR 674.

[78] *Ibid*, at p 680. Cf the position in relation to criminal liability, discussed below, at p 118.

PARTICULAR PROBLEMS RE STATEMENTS

One of the most likely ways for tortious liability to arise in a situation of agency is in relation to statements. We have already seen that care needs to be taken in this area as regards the relationship between the concepts of 'course of employment' and 'authority'. Some other aspects of the law on liability for statements also raise particular problems.

There are three types of action that may be brought in tort for misstatement: (a) deceit; (b) negligent misstatement, under *Hedley Byrne v Heller;*[79] and (c) 'negligent' misrepresentation under s 2(1) of the Misrepresentation Act 1967. All three depend to some extent on the knowledge of the party making the statement. In relation to deceit, it must be a statement of fact (not opinion or law), made with knowledge that it is untrue, or with reckless disregard for the truth.[80] For *Hedley Byrne* there must be a failure to take reasonable care in making the statement. For s 2(1) of the Misrepresentation Act 1967 there will be liability where the maker of a statement of fact which induces a contract cannot prove that they had reasonable grounds to believe that it was true (and did so believe up until the time of any contract made in reliance on it). What is the position if the state of knowledge as between principal and agent is not equal? That is, either the principal knows the statement is untrue and the agent does not, or vice versa.

This issue has been considered in relation to the tort of deceit. A statement made by an agent who knows that it is untrue will, provided that it is made with authority, or ratified, render the principal liable on the basis of vicarious liability, as discussed above.[81] Equally, if the agent is specifically authorised to make a statement the principal knows to be untrue, the principal will be directly liable (whether or not the agent was aware of the falsity of the statement).[82] More difficulty arises where the agent innocently, but without the principal's knowledge or approval, makes a statement the principal knows to be untrue,[83] or where the principal makes a statement which the agent knows to be untrue.[84] The Court of Appeal ruled in *Armstrong v Strain*[85] that in neither of these cases is the principal liable. To hold otherwise would have been, in the view of Devlin J, to 'add an innocent state of mind to an innocent state of mind and get as a result a dishonest state of mind'.

---

[79] [1964] AC 465.

[80] *Derry v Peek* (1889) 14 App Cas 337.

[81] *Hern v Nichols* (1701) 1 Salk 289; *Briess v Wolley* [1954] AC 333.

[82] *Ludgater v Love* (1881) 44 LT 694.

[83] *Cornfoot v Fowke* (1840) 6 M&W 358.

[84] *Anglo-Scottish Beet Sugar Corporation Ltd v Spalding UDC* [1937] 2 KB 607.

[85] [1951] 1 TLR 856.

Turning to s 2(1) of the Misrepresentation Act 1967, this imposes liability where a false statement of fact is made by one party to a contract to the other, which has the effect of inducing a contract. Unless the person can prove that they had reasonable grounds to believe that the statement was true up until the time the contract was made, they will be liable in the same way as if the statement had been made fraudulently. There is no doubt that statements of this kind made by an agent who is acting on the instructions, or with the authority, of a principal, will be regarded as statements made by the principal, rendering the principal liable on that basis. The standard position is illustrated by *Howard Marine Dredging v Ogden & Sons*.[86] In this case the agent of the defendants (who was also an employee) made a representation as to the deadweight capacity of a barge. In doing so he relied on an incorrect figure which appeared in the usually authoritative Lloyds Register. He had, however, also seen the correct figure in the shipping documents. It was held that the agent did not have reasonable grounds for believing the truth of the statement, and therefore his principal was liable under s 2(1) of the Misrepresentation Act. As with deceit, however, the issue will arise as to what the situation should be where either the agent makes a statement which the agent reasonably believes to be true, but the principal knows is untrue, or the principal innocently makes a statement in relation to which the agent is in possession of information which means that the agent could not argue reasonable grounds for belief in its truth.

In *Gosling v Anderson*[87] it was suggested that there was no need in relation to actions under s 2(1) for the plaintiff to establish that the maker of the statement was personally aware of the information which meant that there were no reasonable grounds for believing it to be true. In other words, the view was that the decision in *Armstrong v Strain* was limited to deceit, and did not apply to the action under the 1967 Act. Bowstead, in referring to this issue, comments that 'although this section uses the analogy of fraud in imposing liability, it seems that the fraud rules as to division of ingredients will not be applied'.[88] This conclusion must be reconsidered, however, in the light of the Court of Appeal's approach to s 2(1) in *Royscot Trust Ltd v Rogerson*.[89] The main issue before the court in this case was the measure of damages to be applied under s 2(1). The Court of Appeal, taking a view contrary to that of most commentators, held that the measure of damages should be identical to that available

---

[86] [1978] 1 QB 574.
[87] [1972] 223 EG 1743.
[88] *Op cit*, at p 396, n 47.
[89] [1991] 3 All ER 294.

for the tort of deceit. The main reason for coming to this conclusion was the wording of s 2(1) which makes liability conditional on the situation being that 'the person making the representation would be liable to damages in respect thereof had the misrepresentation been made fraudulently'. This is often referred to as the 'fiction of fraud'. The Court of Appeal rejected the suggestion that this concept was 'misconceived'. On the contrary, it felt that the plain wording of the section meant that actions under s 2(1) had to be treated in exactly the same way as actions for deceit. As had been noted, the primary concern of the Court of Appeal in this case was the issue of the measure of damages. Once, however, a particular approach to the relationship between actions for deceit and actions under s 2(1) has been established, based on the presumption that the same rules ought to apply to both actions, this does have significant implications for the situation where a principal has greater knowledge than an agent who has made a false statement inducing a contract, or vice versa. If the decision in *Royscot* is to be taken as indicating the current approach, then it seems that the principal will only be liable where the agent has no reasonable grounds for believing the truth of the false statement. If the agent reasonably believes it to be true, but the principal knows otherwise, the principal will nevertheless not be liable unless the principal was aware that the agent was making the particular statement in question.

The third type of liability for misstatements is that which arises under the tort of negligence, as developed from the decision in *Hedley Byrne v Heller*.[90] This action is broader than that under s 2(1) of the Misrepresentation Act 1967, in that it is not dependent on the statement inducing a contract, nor on it being a statement of fact. What is necessary, however, is that there should be a duty of care between the person making the statement and the person acting on it. The person acting on it must then have acted in a way that has given rise to a loss. For the principal to be liable for statements made by the agent, there will have to be a duty of care, either directly between the principal and the third party, or between the agent and the third party, with the agent acting within actual or ostensible authority. The basis of the existence of a duty of care under the *Hedley Byrne* category of negligence, has been the subject of extensive debate and consideration by the House of Lords over the past 30 years. Because the liability that arises under this heading is for pure economic loss, it has generally been felt that the test for the existence of a duty should be somewhat stricter than that which applies in relation to the standard tort of negligence derived from *Donoghue v Stevenson*.[91] The speeches in *Hedley Byrne* itself pointed to the need for a

---

[90] [1964] AC 465.
[91] [1932] AC 562.

'special relationship' between the maker of the statement and the plaintiff. This has often been repeated, but as a test of when a duty of care exists, it begs the question, since the identification of those factors which will render a relationship 'special' is just as difficult as identifying the situations where it is appropriate for a duty to arise in the first place.

Another test which has been used is to ask whether it was reasonable for the plaintiff to rely on the maker of the statement. This will bring into play issues such as the situation in which the statement was made, the extent to which the maker of the statement holds themselves out as an expert, and whether the person making the statement is in the business of giving advice to others. The current approach is to be found in the House of Lords' decision in *Caparo v Dickman*.[92] The House adopted a fairly restrictive approach to the situations where a duty would be held to arise, based on the idea of there being a close 'proximity' between the maker of the statement and the person relying on it. This means that a duty is only likely to arise where the maker of the statement knows who is going to be relying on it, and is aware of the use to which it will be put. The House was reluctant to lay down any more detailed principles, preferring to suggest that the law should develop in a 'pragmatic' way, guided by previous case law on the existence of such a duty in particular situations. Several of the speeches reject the idea of considering whether the maker of the statement had undertaken a 'voluntary assumption of responsibility' as being helpful in deciding the issue.[93] This has, however, been given a new lease of life by the comments of Lord Goff in *Henderson v Merrett Syndicates*,[94] where he suggested that 'assumption of responsibility' lies at the heart of the *Hedley Byrne* decision.[95] Although *Henderson* was concerned with broader issues of liability for economic loss, and not primarily liability for statements, Lord Goff's comments will need to be borne in mind as a gloss on the approach suggested by *Caparo*. 'Proximity' will continue to be the dominant consideration, but 'assumption of responsibility' may again be regarded as a relevant factor in deciding whether the required proximity exists.

Turning to the particular situation of the liability of a principal for an agent's negligent misstatements, it would seem that it is enough if the required proximity is established either between the agent and the third party, or between the principal and third party. Provided that either of

---

[92] [1990] 1 All ER 568.

[93] Eg Lord Roskill, at p 582.

[94] [1994] 3 All ER 506. This case is also discussed in connection with the liability of sub-agents: see Chapter 3, at p 56.

[95] *Ibid*, at p 521.

these relationships establishes a duty of care in relation to negligent misstatements, then the principal will be liable for any such statements made by the agent, provided that they are made with authority.

The personal liability of the *agent* for misstatements of this kind is considered in Chapter 5.[96]

CRIMINAL LIABILITY

There are certain circumstances where a principal will be criminally liable for offences committed by an agent. The position here is slightly different to that considered in the rest of this chapter, in that the principal is not in these circumstances brought into a legal relationship with a third party, and found to have obligations towards that third party (as with contract and tort), but is held liable *vis-à-vis* the State for the commission of a criminal offence. The consequences are the imposition of a penalty, most probably in the form of a fine or imprisonment, rather than the payment of compensation, in the form of damages.

There are three possible ways in which a principal may become criminally liable through the actions of an action. First, the principal may simply use an innocent agent as an unwitting means of committing a criminal offence. Secondly, where an agent commits a criminal offence in the course of carrying out his duties as an agent, the principal may be held responsible for this, and thus *vicariously* liable. Thirdly, in some situations the actions of an agent may be deemed to be the actions of the principal: if these constitute a criminal offence, the principal will be *directly* liable for the offence concerned. This type of liability is particularly important where the principal is a corporate body, such as a limited company. These three situations will be considered in turn, and then some particular problems relating to corporate liability will be discussed.

Innocent agency

If a principal gives an agent a package containing a bomb, and the agent delivers this, as instructed, to a third party, with the result that when the bomb explodes the third party is killed, the principal will be liable for murder, despite the fact that it was the actions of the agent which were the immediate cause of death. Similarly, where a principal, as part of a fraudulent enterprise, entrusts an agent with forged documents of title,

---

[96] At p 141.

and the agent uses these to obtain money from a third party, the principal will be liable for obtaining property by deception, contrary to s 15 of the Theft Act 1978. Both the 'obtaining' and the 'deception' will be achieved through by acts of the agent, but these can be attributed to the principal, and combined with the principal's dishonest intention to fulfill all the elements of the offence.

In such situations, the agent, if totally ignorant of the principal's unlawful purposes, will be innocent of any offence. The only liability will be that of the principal. On the other hand, an agent who is aware of what is going on, will be liable as either an accessory or a conspirator, jointly with the principal.

Vicarious liability

As with the law of tort, vicarious liability in the criminal law arises where a wrongful act is committed by the agent, without the approval of the principal, but the principal is nevertheless held responsible. A good example of this is *Coppen v Moore (No 2)*.[97] A shop owner had issued instructions that ham was not to be sold under any specific name indicating its origin. An employee, sold some American ham as Scotch ham. This constituted an offence under the Merchandise Marks Act 1887, s 2(2), in that it amounted to the sale of goods under a false trade description. The court took the view that the wording of the statute made it clear that parliament must have intended that an employer should be responsible for the acts of an employee which fell within the course of employment, even though such acts had been expressly prohibited. The act of selling the ham was clearly within the course of employment, and the employer was therefore responsible. The employee was, of course, acting as agent for the employer in relation to the contract of sale, so the case must be taken as indicating the law as between principal and agent, as much as between employer and employee.

Vicarious liability of this type will generally only arise where the offence in question is one of strict liability, with no requirement for the prosecution to prove any particular mental element in relation to the defendant. If the definition of the offence contains a *mens rea* element, then this will have to be proved against the principal, and thus the liability will become direct, rather than vicarious. This means that the vast majority of situations where there is potential for a principal being vicariously liable for a criminal offence, is where the offence is statutory.

---

97   [1898] 2 QB 306.

At common law, strict liability is rare, but does exist in relation to public nuisance,[98] criminal libel,[99] and contempt of court. The first two of these are, as Fridman has pointed out,[100] of little theoretical or practical importance: the third will be considered later in this section.

The finding that a statute creates strict liability depends on a close analysis of its wording, and an attempt to determine the intention of the legislature.[101] The presence of words such as 'intentionally', 'recklessly', 'maliciously', or 'knowingly' in the definition of the offence will preclude a finding of strict liability. The courts will, however, also consider the context of the offence, and in particular whether it can be said to be concerned with 'real crime' (murder, theft, etc) or simply 'regulatory offences' (parking, trading standards, control of pollution). In relation to the former, the courts will tend to presume a requirement of *mens rea*, and in some circumstances to read this into the statute.[102]

A decision that a statute imposes strict liability is not, however, conclusive that vicarious liability will be imposed. Much of our law relating to road traffic offences involves strict liability, but it is inconceivable that a principal could be found vicariously liable for an agent who has been arrested for a drink/driving offence, simply because the agent was at the time engaged upon business on behalf of the principal.[103] However, an employer has been held liable where an employee was driving a vehicle which did not comply with the construction and use regulations.[104] The offence was one of 'using' the vehicle, and the view was taken that the employer was in the circumstances 'using' the vehicle through the agency of the employee. This illustrates that it is important to consider the precise nature of the offence, and whether the actions which comprise it can properly be said to be the responsibility of the principal, as well as the agent. As has been pointed out by Leigh,[105] this can lead to the creation of a kind of judicial 'dictionary' whereby the possibility of vicarious liability depends on which words are used in creating it. Thus the words 'sell', 'use', or 'cause' can give rise to vicarious liability, whereas 'permit' (which

---

[98] *R v Stephens* (1866) LR 1 QB 702.

[99] Whether blasphemous (*R v Lemon* [1979] 1 All ER 898), or defamatory (*R v Wicks* (1936) 25 Cr App R 168; *Goldsmith v Pressdram* [1977] 2 All ER 557).

[100] *Op cit*, p 304.

[101] For a full discussion of the issue see, eg, Smith and Hogan, *Criminal Law*, 7th edn, pp 103–114.

[102] Eg *Sweet v Parsley* [1970] AC 132.

[103] *Cf Meridian Global Funds Management Asia Ltd v Securities Commission* [1995] 3 All ER 918, at p 928, where Lord Hoffmann makes a similar point in relation to manslaughter.

[104] *Green v Burnett* [1955] 1 QB 78.

[105] *Strict and Vicarious Liability*, Sweet & Maxwell 1982, p 47.

implies knowledge) is unlikely to do so. Such an approach runs the risk of the court making criminal liability depend on fine distinctions of meaning which may not have been intended by parliament, and may be criticised on the basis that it is a technical rather than policy-based approach. Nevertheless, it remains an important element in the courts consideration of these types of liability.[106]

Even where the statutory language creating the offence is found to be apt to give rise to vicarious liability, it is not uncommon for parliament to have provided an 'escape route' by means of a 'due diligence' defence. Thus, the principal will be able to escape liability by proving, on the balance of probabilities, that all reasonable steps had been taken to prevent the commission of the offence by the agent. Such a defence must be specifically included, however. The courts will not assume that parliament intended it to be available unless it is specifically stated.[107]

The possibility of vicarious liability in relation to an offence requiring *mens rea* appears to be limited to situations involving delegation of responsibility under a statutory licence. In the leading case on this topic, *Allen v Whitehead*,[108] the owner of a cafe licensed by a local authority was found to have delegated the running of it to a manager. The manager allowed prostitutes to meet at the cafe. The owner was charged with the offence of 'knowingly' allowing prostitutes to gather there. Despite the fact that there was clear evidence that the owner had given the manager instructions to keep the prostitutes away, and had put up notices to this effect, he was convicted. He, as licensee, had delegated his responsibilities under the licence to the manager, but nevertheless remained vicariously liable for the manager's actions. Since the manager had 'knowingly' allowed the prostitutes on to the premises, the owner was also liable. He was infected with the manager's *mens rea*. This does not mean, however, that a principal who is a licensee will be responsible for all criminal acts committed by an agent. In *Vane v Yiannopoullos*[109] it was held that the holder of a liquor licence was not criminally liable for the actions of an unsupervised waitress, who had served drinks to customers in breach of the terms of the licence.[110] It could not be said that the principal had in this case delegated responsibilities under the licence to his agent. It is in fact only where the principal has effectively delegated *all* responsibility that the approach taken in *Allen v Whitehead* will be appropriate. In such a situation, as the court in *Allen v Whitehead*

---

[106] See, for example, the Divisional Court's approach to the word 'supply' in *Tesco Stores v Brent London BC* [1993] 2 All ER 718.

[107] *Tesco Stores v Brent London BC* [1993] 2 All ER 718, at p 720.

[108] [1930] 1 KB 211.

[109] [1965] AC 486, [1964] 3 All ER 820.

[110] See also *R v Winson* [1969] 1 QB 371, [1968] 1 All ER 197.

pointed out, it would render the care taken to decide who should be awarded a licence superfluous, if it was possible for the licence-holder to then delegate all responsibility, and thus render himself immune from prosecution for breaches of the terms of the licence.

Before leaving the area of vicarious liability we should note the position where, by breaching the terms of court order, an agent acts in a way amounting to contempt of court. To what extent is a principal liable for such a breach? This issue was reconsidered by the House of Lords in *Re Supply of Ready Mixed Concrete (No 2)*.[111] The Restrictive Practices Court had made orders restraining, *inter alia*, price-fixing arrangements between firms involved in the supply of ready-mixed concrete. Subsequently, local managers employed by various companies, in contravention of express instructions issued to them by their employers, entered into such agreements. The question before the House of Lords was whether such agreements amounted to contempt of the order of the Restrictive Practices Court by the employers. It was accepted that it was not necessary for any intention to commit contempt to be shown in order for liability to arise. The employers, however, relied on the approach taken by Lord Wilberforce in *Heatons Transport (St Helens) Ltd v Transport and General Workers Union*,[112] the facts of which have been given elsewhere.[113] He had said that the critical test of the liability of an employer or principal for contempt resulting from the actions of a servant or agent, was whether the servant or agent was 'acting on behalf of, *and within the scope of the authority conferred by*, the master or principal'.[114] In that case, therefore, it had been necessary to determine whether the union's shop stewards still had authority from the union to organise the 'blacking' of ships, or whether such authority had effectively been withdrawn. The House of Lords held that the authority continued, and that the union was therefore responsible for the shop stewards' acts. In the *Ready Mixed Concrete* case, however, it was accepted that the local managers had neither actual nor ostensible authority to make the agreements. Nevertheless, it was held that, in doing so, they were still acting in the course of their employment. On this basis, distinguishing *Heatons Transport (St Helens) Ltd v Transport and General Workers Union*, the House of Lords ruled that the managers' employers could be liable for the agreements which they had made, and thus guilty of contempt. In coming to this conclusion the House approved the similar view taken by Warrington J in *Stancomb v Trowbridge UDC*.[115] The result is that in relation to this type of contempt,

---

[111] [1995] 1 All ER 135.

[112] [1972] 3 All ER 101; [1972] 3 WLR 431.

[113] Above, p 4.

[114] [1972] 3 All ER 101, at 109; [1973] AC 15, at 99 (emphasis added).

[115] [1910] 2 Ch 190.

the position as to vicarious liability differs as between employers and principals. Whereas an employer will be liable if the employee is acting in the course of employment, even though without authority, and 'in dereliction of duty',[116] a principal who is not an employer will only be liable if the agent has acted with either actual or ostensible authority.

Direct liability

In some cases, a principal's criminal liability may not depend on establishing any wrongful act on the part of an agent. As with vicarious liability, this is most likely to be the case with statutory offences, based on strict liability. If, for example, the principal is engaged in a business involving the use of water which becomes contaminated by some manufacturing process, and some of that water is discharged into a river, the principal may be said to have 'caused' the pollution of the river, without the need to show any particular wrongful act on the part of an agent. That is a simplified version of the facts of the case of *Alphacell v Woodward*.[117] As a matter of fact, it was the acts or omissions of the principal's agents or employees which must have led to the pollution, but since the offence was based on 'causing', rather than 'knowingly causing' the pollution, there was no need to investigate this in detail. The acts of the agents were the acts of the principal for these purposes. The theory is thus one of 'identification': the agent is 'identified' with the principal, and his acts or omissions are deemed to be those of the principal. This analysis is not, of course, peculiar to criminal liability. Indeed, it may be said to lie at the heart of the concept of agency itself, and in particular to contractual obligations flowing from agency.

Corporations

Where the principal is a corporation, rather than a real person, it may, of course, be vicariously or directly liable for criminal offences in the ways described in ss 2 and 3, above. It is also possible, however, for a corporation to be *directly* liable for offences requiring *mens rea*. Once again the dominant theory is one of 'identification'. The prosecution will need to show that the agent had the required *mens rea*, and that, for these purposes the mental state of the agent can be identified with that of the corporation (which being inanimate can have no mind of its own). For the last 20 years this area has been dominated by the decision of the

---

116 [1995] 1 All ER 135, at 156, *per* Lord Nolan.

117 [1972] AC 824. See also *National Rivers Authority v Yorkshire Water Services* [1995] 1 All ER 225.

House of Lords in *Tesco Supermarkets Ltd v Nattrass*.[118] The case concerned an offence of the Trade Descriptions Act 1968, s 11(2), of 'offering to supply goods' with a misleading indication as to the price at which they were available. The manager of Tesco supermarket had, by mistake, allowed advertisements of a 'special offer' to be displayed even though no items were available in the store at the special price. Tesco Ltd were charged with the offence, but relied on a 'due diligence' defence contained in s 24(2). This required them to establish that the offence was due to the 'default of another person', and that they had taken 'all reasonable precautions and exercised all due diligence' to avoid the commission of the offence. There was no doubt that the first part of this test could be satisfied, in that the default was that of the manager or those working under him. The main question before the House was whether for the purposes of the second part of the defence, the failure of the manager to exercise due diligence had to be attributed to the company, or whether it was enough that the company itself had established procedures which ought to have prevented what in fact occurred. To answer this question, the House of Lords considered whether the manager could be 'identified' with the company for these purposes. Their conclusion was that he could not. Adopting the approach taken in earlier cases, such as *Lennard's Carrying Co Ltd v Asiatic Petroleum Co Ltd*,[119] and *Bolton Engineering Co Ltd v Graham & Sons Ltd*[120] they held that the manager could only be identified with the company for these purposes if he could be said to be part of its 'directing mind and will'. This in effect meant directors, or senior managers. A local store manager was not sufficiently high in the hierarchy of the company to fulfill this criteria, and so his lack of care could not be attributed to the company. The company was therefore able to rely on the defence in s 24(1).

Although this case was concerned with a specific statutory defence, it has subsequently been taken as establishing the general principle that agents (or employees) acting on behalf of a company will only infect their principal (or employer) with the *mens rea* necessary to establish criminal liability, if they are part of the 'directing mind and will' of the company, as determined in *Tesco v Nattrass*. Two recent decisions have, however, cast some doubt on whether this test is sufficiently subtle to deal with all situations. In *Tesco Stores Ltd v Brent London Borough Council*[121] the Divisional Court was considering the liability of Tesco's

---

[118] [1972] AC 153, [1971] 2 All ER 127.
[119] [1915] AC 705.
[120] [1957] 1 QB 159, [1956] 3 All ER 624.
[121] [1993] 2 All ER 718.

for the supply of a video cassette classified as suitable only for those over 18 to a person aged 14, contrary to s 11 of the Video Recordings Act 1984. The physical acts amounting to the supply had been those of a cashier in the Tesco store, and it was accepted that she had reasonable grounds to believe that the person to whom she supplied the video was under 18. Tesco, however, sought to rely on s 11(2) of the Act, which provides a defence where 'the accused neither knew or had reasonable grounds to believe that the person concerned had not attained' the required age. The question therefore was whether the knowledge or belief of the cashier could be imputed to Tesco, the company itself being 'the accused'. Tesco argued that on the basis of *Tesco v Nattrass* the cashier was not part of the 'directing mind and will' of the company, and so her mental state should not be imputed to it. The Divisional Court refused to accept this, ruling that there was a material distinction between a 'due diligence' defence based on the company's procedures, and the defence here which was based on knowledge and information. Moreover, it was clear that companies were expected to have potential liability under s 11, and yet it would be:

absurd to suppose that those who manage a vast company would have any knowledge or any information as to the age of a casual purchaser of a video film. It is the employee that sells the film at the check-out point who will have knowledge or reasonable grounds for belief. It is her knowledge or reasonable grounds that are relevant.[122]

As a result, Tesco were not able to rely on the defence, and were liable for the supply.

This decision indicates that the 'directing mind and will' approach cannot be used as the test in relation to all issues of imputing the *mens rea* of an agent to a principal. Attention needs to be paid to the precise context in which any mental element is operating. This theme was strongly reinforced by the Privy Council in *Meridian Global Funds Management Asia Ltd v Securities Commission*.[123] The case concerned a complex fraud, concerning the take-over of one company by another. The particular question before the court was whether the company whose employees had perpetrated the fraud could be imputed with their knowledge of events, so as to make the company in breach of a requirement under s 20 of the New Zealand Securities Amendment Act 1988 to give notice of particular holdings of shares as soon as it was aware of them. The company argued that the employees concerned were not part of its 'directing mind and will', and that their knowledge should not be imputed to it. Lord Hoffmann, who delivered the opinion of the Privy Council, analysed the history of the concept of 'directing mind and

---

[122] *Ibid*, at p 721, *per* Staughton LJ.
[123] [1995] 3 All ER 918.

will', and demonstrated that it should not be used as the sole means of determining when the mental state of an agent or employee should be imputed to a corporation. Much depends on the context, which will require a determination of what is the relevant 'attribution rule' to apply. In some cases this will be the 'primary rules of attribution', based on the corporation's constitution, which will give certain decision-making powers to, eg, the Board of Directors. More generally the corporation will be affected by the general rules relating to agency and vicarious liability, by which acts done within authority, or the course of employment, will make the company liable. In relation to criminal offences, however, which are generally defined in terms of the *actus reus* and *mens rea* of human beings, it will often be necessary to decide on an offence by offence basis what the appropriate rule of attribution should be. This is primarily a matter of statutory interpretation:

> [G]iven that [the offence] was intended to apply to accompany, how was it intended to apply? Whose act (or knowledge, or state of mind) was *for this purpose* intended to count as the act of the company.[124]

The task is not therefore primarily the 'metaphysical' one of determining who constitutes a company's directing mind and will, but one of construction, with a view to determining the appropriate rule of attribution for a particular offence. This will take into account the formulation of the offence, and the policy which may be identified as lying behind it. Was it intended that companies should be liable for the offence? If so, at what level of activity should the company be affixed with responsibility? Very often this may be determined by asking whether the actions of an agent fell within the agent's authority. Thus in the present case it was appropriate that, in the case of the purchase of shares, the knowledge of the person who made the acquisition, with the authority of the company, should count as the knowledge of the company. This will not always be the correct test, however, and Lord Hoffmann emphasised that:

> It is a question of construction in each case as to whether the particular rule requires that the knowledge that an act has been done, or the state of mind with which it was done, should be attributed to the company.[125]

This more flexible approach to the attribution of criminal liability in relation to the behaviour of agents has much to commend it. On the other hand, it will tend to contribute uncertainty, in that it will be to a certain extent unpredictable how a court will interpret the appropriate 'rule of attribution' for any particular offence.

---

[124] *Ibid*, at p 924 (original emphasis).
[125] *Ibid*, at p 928.

CHAPTER 5

AGENT AND THIRD PARTY

INTRODUCTION: THE GENERAL RULE

The main object of agency arrangements is to facilitate some aspect of the legal relationship between the principal and a third party. It follows from this that the general rule as regards the legal rights and liabilities between agent and third party is that there are none. Assuming the agent carries out the obligations imposed satisfactorily, and the relationship between principal and third party does not break down in any way, then the agent should disappear from view. Such legal rights and obligations as the agent has in that situation will exist *vis-à-vis* the principal, rather than the third party. These have been discussed at length in Chapter 3.

This is, however, only the general rule, and there is a range of situations where the agent will in fact have the possibility of suing, or being sued by, the third party. This may be because of the express or implied terms of the contract with the third party; the actions of the agent; or the effect of statutory rules. The rest of this chapter explores the situations where such rights and liabilities arise.

AGENT'S RIGHTS AND LIABILITIES ON THE CONTRACT

The intention of the parties

One of the main considerations here is the intention of the parties. If it is clear that the agent and third party agreed there should be rights and liabilities between them in relation to any contract that is made, notwithstanding any rights and liabilities *vis-à-vis* the principal, then the courts will give effect to that intention. The clearest way in which this can be done is by an express agreement to that effect. In the absence of that, the courts will have to interpret the contract itself to see whether such an intention can be implied. Brandon J in *The Swan*,[1] pointed out that the intention of the parties is to be gathered from the nature of the

---

[1]   [1968] 1 Lloyds Rep 5, at p 12.

contract, its terms, and the surrounding circumstances. Intention is not subjective.

> The intention for which the Court looks is an objective intention, based on what two reasonable businessmen making a contract of that nature, in those terms and in those surrounding circumstances, must be taken to have intended.

In *The Swan* itself, the defendant, JD Rodger, owned a boat which he hired to his company, JD Rodger Ltd. The company instructed the plaintiffs, who were ship-repairers, to do work on the boat. The orders for this work were partly oral, communicated by JD Rodger, and partly on company notepaper, over the signature 'JD Rodger, Director.' Accounts for the work were sent to the company, but it could not pay. The plaintiffs therefore tried to sue JD Rodger personally. The contract had clearly been made through his agency. Did that mean he, as agent, had no liability under it? It was held it was natural in the circumstances for the plaintiffs to assume that the owner of the boat would take responsibility for work carried out on it. In this case, therefore, the fact that the agent was also the owner of the property which was the subject of the contract was an important element in the decision in favour of making the agent liable. Indeed, the court clearly suggests that if this had not been the case, the decision would have gone the other way. The case obviously has considerable importance for 'one-person' companies, and indicates that the corporate structure will not necessarily provide a defence where contracts are made on behalf of the company in relation to property which in fact belongs to the person who is acting as agent for the company.

In some cases the form of signature was regarded as significant so that to sign 'as solicitors',[2] or indeed 'as director',[3] would have been regarded as merely 'descriptive' and not indicating any intention to avoid legal liability. To sign 'on behalf of' or 'per pro',[4] however, would be regarded as 'representative', and an indication that the signatory was not intended to attract any personal liability. In *Gadd v Houghton*,[5] for example, the use of the phrase 'on account of' X in a contract for the purchase of goods, was taken to indicate that there was no intention to incur personal liability. And in *Universal Steam Navigation Co Ltd v J McKelvie & Co*[6] a similar effect was claimed for the phrase 'as agents'. As we have seen, however, in *The Swan* the form of the signature was not regarded as having any overriding significance. More recent case law

---

2   *Burrell v Jones* (1819) 3 B&Ald 47.
3   *McCollin v Gilpin* (1881) 6 QBD 516.
4   *Downman v Williams* (1845) 7 QB 103.
5   (1876) 1 Ex D 357.
6   [1923] AC 492.

suggests that the courts are no longer so likely to put weight on this aspect of the contract.[7] It is simply one factor to be looked at in trying to determine the intention of the parties.

In three particular situations, however, there is a presumption that an agent who has put their signature to a document is liable personally on it. First, an agent who has executed a deed will be liable on it, whether or not it is stated that the execution is undertaken as agent for someone else.[8] Second, an agent who signs a negotiable instrument must use clear words (something more than simply 'as agent') to avoid personal liability.[9] Third, an officer of a registered company who signs any bill of exchange, promissory note, endorsement, cheque or order for money or goods, without the name of the company appearing on the document in legible characters, will, by virtue of s 349(4) of the Companies Act 1985, be personally liable.[10]

Custom

Custom, or trade usage may in some cases mean that an agent is liable or entitled to be sued or to sue on a contract. Unless a clear contrary intention is expressed, the courts will give effect to such a custom. Thus in *Pike v Ongley*[11] the court accepted evidence of a custom in the hop trade whereby a broker who does not identify the principal at the time of the contract is personally liable.[12] The custom must, however, be consistent with the terms of the contract itself. In *Barrow & Bros v Dyster, Nalder & Co*[13] the plaintiffs wished to introduce evidence of a custom of the hide trade in the city of London, whereby brokers could in some circumstances be personally liable on contracts they negotiated. This was rejected, because the contract in this case constituted the brokers as arbitrators of disputes between the contracting parties. It was clearly incompatible with this role that the brokers should also have liability under the contract.

---

7 Eg *Punjab National Bank v De Boinville* [1992] 1 Lloyd's Rep. See also *Phonogram v Lane* [1981] 3 All ER 182, which is discussed below, at p 36, in connection with the situation of the 'non-existent' principal.

8 *Appleton v Binks* (1804) 5 East 148; *Hancock v Hodgson* (1827) 4 Bing 269.

9 Bills of Exchange Act 1882, s 17(1).

10 And may also be fined. Cf *Durham Fancy Goods Ltd v Michael Jackson (Fancy Goods) Ltd* [1968] 2 QB 839.

11 (1887) 18 QBD 708.

12 For further examples, see Bowstead, *op cit*, p 450.

13 (1884) 13 QBD 635.

Undisclosed principal

When the principal is undisclosed, the third party initially thinks that they are dealing solely with the agent. As we have seen in Chapter 4,[14] the principal is in general able to enforce the contract, and will also be liable on it. At the same time, the third party is, not surprisingly, entitled to enforce against the agent, who is the person with whom the third party thought the contract was being made. It is in this situation, where there appears to be alternative liability, that the doctrine of election may become relevant. This is discussed below.[15]

Unidentified principal

The position is less clear in relation to the 'halfway-house' situation where the agent makes it clear that a principal is involved, but does not identify them. Bowstead suggests that the rule *ought* to be that the agent should *prima facie* be liable alongside the principal.[16] That does not, however, seem to be the effect of the current case law. In *N & J Vlassopoulos Ltd v Ney Shipping Ltd (The Santa Carina)*,[17] a telephone order was placed by one broker with another. Both brokers were aware that the other was unlikely to be acting personally, though nothing specific was said about the basis on which the parties were making the contract. It was held that the broker placing the order was not personally liable on the contract. Since this situation was, given the state of mind of the brokers, effectively one of a disclosed but unnamed principal, the case suggests that, at least as far as oral contracts are concerned, the agent has no liability in this situation. There appears to be a dearth of authority on the position where a written contract refers to an unnamed principal. Perhaps the situation is one which simply does not arise with any frequency. Where the contract is in writing it is easier to spell out the exact position of each participant to the transaction. There would seem to be little reason, however, for the *prima facie* rule being any different from that which applies to oral contracts, ie that the agent is not liable.

A case that gives some indication of how this can operate is *Tudor Marine Ltd v Tradax Export*.[18] The documentation here may be said to have been equivocal as to the status of the defendants. At one point they were described as 'charterers', while elsewhere in the charterparty it said that the vessel concerned was chartered 'on behalf of and for account of'

---

14   Above, p 93.
15   At p 144.
16   *Op cit*, p 434. See also Reynolds [1983] CLP 119.
17   [1977] 1 Lloyd's Rep 478
18   [1976] 2 Lloyd's Rep 135.

another firm. A letter, however, which it was agreed should be regarded as forming part of the contract, stated that: 'It is mutually agreed that Charterers are to be ultimately responsible for demurrage payments'.[19] The Court of Appeal held that, whether or not the defendants were acting as agents, they were, as a result of this statement in the letter, personally liable on the charter for the demurrage payments. The fact that this needed arguing indicates that the *prima facie* position would be that the agent is not liable.

Bowstead, in suggesting that the *prima facie* rule ought to be that where the principal is unnamed, the agent is liable, argues that the courts may under the current rule 'stretch' the category of undisclosed principal, and 'classify the principal as undisclosed rather than unnamed in order to secure the liability of the agent'.[20] At the moment, however, such authority as there is leans towards treating the agent acting for an unnamed principal more leniently than one acting for an undisclosed principal, and *prima facie* absolving such an agent from liability on the contract.

Foreign principal

If an agent is acting for a foreign principal, this obviously increases the risks for the third party in terms of the ability to enforce any contract against the principal. This was particularly so during the period when international trade was developing and communications were relatively poor. In this context it is not surprising that the courts developed the approach that there should be a presumption that where an agent is dealing for a foreign principal, the agent should have personal liability on any contract negotiated.[21] In modern times, however, where the improvements in travel and international communication mean that international boundaries are much less significant, such a presumption is much less justifiable. The modern approach to this issue should, therefore, be taken as being more accurately indicated by the approach of the Court of Appeal in *Teheran-Europe Co Ltd v ST Belton (Tractors) Ltd*.[22] In this case, the principal, a company based in what was then known as Persia (now Iran), was not fully identified by the agent. The court therefore treated this as a case of not only a principal who was foreign, but also unnamed (or, *per* Lord Denning, undisclosed). The court was unanimous in its view that the fact that the principal here was

---

19 *Ibid*, at p 145.
20 See above, n 16.
21 See eg *Paterson v Gandasequi* [1812] 15 East 62, and other cases cited by Bowstead, *op cit*, p 435.
22 [1968] 2 QB 545.

based out of the country was only of limited importance in determining the legal rights and liabilities as between the three parties involved.

Developments such as the use of bankers' commercial credits meant that the approach taken in the mid-19th century to these issues was no longer appropriate. As Lord Denning put it:[23]

> In the light of modern usage I think that an undisclosed foreign principal can sue and be sued upon a contract, just as an undisclosed English principal can, save, of course, when the contract on its true construction limits it to the English intermediary and excludes a foreign principal. The fact that the principal is a foreigner is an element to be thrown into the scale on construction, but that is all.

Diplock LJ was more sceptical about the justification for the 19th century usage, but agreed with Lord Denning that it was in any case inappropriate in the modern commercial world. The fact that a principal was foreign while a relevant circumstance in considering whether the agent was intended to be personally liable, would be of particularly minimal importance where, as in the present case, the terms of payment were cash before delivery, and no credit is extended by the third party to the principal.

The present state of the law on this issue, therefore, seems to be that the fact that a principal is based abroad, is simply one factor to be taken into account in trying to assess the intentions of the parties as to who should have liability. It can no longer be said to be the case that the courts will start with a presumption that in such circumstances the agent is always intended to have personal liability.

Position of the agent where there is no principal

Two situations need consideration. First, the situation may be that the 'agent', while purporting to act for a principal, is in fact acting on their own behalf. Second, the agent may intend to act for a principal, but the principal does not in fact exist at the relevant time. This problem is most likely to arise in relation to companies which are in the process of formation.

Where the agent is in fact the principal

The rule here would seem to be that agents who hold themselves out as acting for a principal, will be personally liable on any contract made with a third party. It can be argued that a better way of dealing with such a situation would be to hold the agent liable on a collateral contract,

---

[23] At p 553.

or perhaps on the basis of misrepresentation, for the false statement as to the existence of the principal.[24] There are, however, some, albeit not very clear, authorities which indicate that the agent is to be regarded as simply liable on the contract itself.[25] And indeed, whatever the arguments of principle, it may well be that this is the most efficient way of dealing with the situation. In *Railton v Hodgson*,[26] for example, the defendant ordered from the plaintiffs goods in the name of a firm for whom he had previously worked. The plaintiffs entered the transaction in their books in the name of the firm. The goods were delivered to the defendant, however, and when it transpired that the firm was insolvent, the plaintiffs sued the defendant, and succeeded on the contract. It appeared that the defendant had always intended to have the goods for his own use, and had only used the name of the firm in order to obtain credit. The complication here is that the firm was apparently willing to accept this use of their name in return for a commission on the transaction. Thus, although it is an example of an agent, who is really the principal, being liable on the contract, it might well be a situation where the firm should also have been liable, on the basis of ostensible authority. And the fact that the third party was apparently looking solely to the firm for payment throughout the transaction might have been thought to preclude a subsequent action against the 'agent'.

This certainly seems to be the implication of a more recent example of the courts' approach to this issue: *Gardiner v Heading*.[27] A builder had on previous occasions done work for a company, FGC, which had been introduced to him by H. H had therefore acted as agent for FGC. When H asked the builder to undertake further work, the builder assumed that this was again being requested on behalf of FGC. In fact, H, although he was aware of the builder's mistake, was on this occasion acting on his own behalf. The question was whether H could be held personally liable on the contract, when the builder had, up until the time when payment was requested, thought that he was dealing with FGC. Scrutton LJ had no doubt that the builder should be able to sue H. As he commented:

> If a man who contracts with another thinking he is a principal, may, on finding he is in truth an agent, sue the real principal, why should not the reverse hold good also? Why should not a man who contracts with another, thinking he is an agent, sue him when he finds out that he is the real principal? There seems to be no reason

---

24 See eg Bowstead, *op cit*, pp 474–5.
25 Eg *Railton v Hodgson* (1804) 4 Taunt 576n.
26 *Ibid*.
27 [1928] 2 KB 284.

why he should not, provided the supposed agent has not expressly contracted as agent so as to exclude his liability as a principal party to that contract.

It was clearly regarded as important in this case, that the builder did not give exclusive credit to FGC. The court's view of the facts was that the builder had not looked solely to FGC for payment, so as to exclude the supposed agent from all liability. It may be, therefore, that the decision in *Railton v Hodgson* would not now go the same way.

Where the agent has purported to be acting for a specific named principal when, in fact this is not the case, there may also be the possibility, if the third party suffers a loss thereby, of an action for breach of the implied warranty of authority (which is discussed below), or even, if a deliberate intention to mislead can be shown, for the tort of deceit. Deceit is generally the most powerful action, because of the extent of damages which are recoverable, whereas in relation to breach of the implied warranty the quantum is limited by what could have been recovered from the purported principal in an action on the contract. In some cases, however, for example where the third party is seeking specific performance, the most attractive option will be to try to enforce the contract which has been agreed against the purported agent.

One reason for allowing an action on the contract in these situations is that the agent who, while purporting to act for a principal, in fact acts personally, will be entitled to enforce any subsequent contract. The desirability of 'mutuality' of action therefore suggests that the agent should be personally liable. A leading authority on the ability of the agent who purports to act for a principal nevertheless being able to sue in person is *Schmaltz v Avery*.[28] This decision has been heavily criticised by Bowstead,[29] but nevertheless appears to remain good law. The plaintiffs had signed a charterparty in the form 'G Schmaltz & Co as agents of the freighter'. When they subsequently tried to take action on the charter, the defendants argued that the way in which they had signed precluded a personal action. The plaintiffs, having indicated that they were acting for someone else (albeit that that person was not specified) should not be allowed to claim that they were in fact the principal, rather than agents. The court rejected this argument. As Patteson J put it:

> [T]here is no contradiction of the charterparty if the plaintiff can be considered as filling two characters, namely those of agent and principal. A man cannot in strict propriety of speech be said to be

---

[28] (1851) 16 QB 655.
[29] *Op cit*, pp 477–9.

agent to himself. Yet, in a contract of this description, we see no absurdity in saying that he might fill both characters; that he might contract as agent for the freighter whoever that freighter might turn out to be, and might still adopt that character of freighter himself if he chose.[30]

It was clearly significant that the court did not feel that the defendant was in any way prejudiced by the plaintiffs' action. The defendant could not, for example, have been relying on the solvency of the freighter, 'since the freighter is admitted to have been unknown to him, and he did not think it necessary to enquire who he was'.[31] If the identity of the principal were significant, or if it were clear that the third party would not be prepared to contract with the agent as principal, then the position would be different, as it is where an undisclosed principal wishes to enforce a contract.[32] In the absence of such considerations, however, the agent may step into the shoes of an unnamed principal, and sue the third party on the contract.

Principal non-existent

As noted above, this situation is most likely to arise in relation to companies which are in the process of formation. The issue is the extent to which pre-incorporation contracts, reportedly made on behalf of the company, can be enforced by or against the professed agent. We have already considered this issue (above, Chapter 2).[33] It was noted there that the company once incorporated is not able to ratify the actions of the person who was trying to act on its behalf. That person's own legal position is governed by both common law and statutory rules.

The leading case on the common law position is *Kelner v Baxter*.[34] K had contracted to sell goods to a group of people who indicated that they were purchasing 'on behalf of the proposed Gravesend Royal Alexandra Hotel Co Ltd'. The contract was made prior to the incorporation of the company. It was held that the promoters of the company were personally liable on this contract. The position as regards contracts of this kind, is now in fact governed by s 36(4) of the Companies Act 1985. This incorporates into English law the European rules governing this area, as set out in an EEC Directive (68/151). This was originally given effect by the European Communities Act 1972 s 9(2). Section 36(4) states:

---

[30] *Ibid*, at p 663.
[31] *Ibid*, at p 662.
[32] See p 96.
[33] See p 27.
[34] (1866) LR 2 CP 174.

Where a contract purports to be made by a company, or by a person as agent for a company, at a time when the company has not yet been formed, then subject to any agreement to the contrary, the contract shall have effect as a contract entered into by the person purporting to act for the company or as agent for it, and he shall be personally liable on the contract accordingly.

Two points should be noted about this provision. First, it applies only where there is no 'agreement to the contrary'. It is always possible, therefore, for the parties to agree some different distribution of liabilities from that provided for by the section. Second, the section only deals on its face with the liability of those who act, or purport to act, for the company. It says nothing about whether they can enforce the agreement against the third party. This issue is one that needs to be explored further.

The common law position as regards the agent's ability to enforce the contract was governed by the case of *Newborne v Sensolid*.[35] In this case Leopold Newborne was forming a company which was to be known as 'Leopold Newborne (London) Ltd'. He entered into an agreement on the contract form which was headed with the company's name, address, etc for the sale of tinned ham to the defendant. The agreement was signed 'Leopold Newborne (London) Ltd'. The defendants refused to accept delivery. The plaintiff originally sued in the company's name, but when it was discovered that the company had not been registered at the time of the contract, the plaintiff tried to sue in his own name instead.

The Court of Appeal held that he could not succeed. They reached this decision by looking carefully at the form in which the agreement had been signed. They felt this indicated that Newborne had not purported to sell as either principal or agent. The only contract, if there was any at all, was with the company. Since the company was not in existence at the time of the contract, this meant that the 'contract' was a nullity. At common law, therefore, the indication was that the agent could not enforce a pre-incorporation contract of this type. When the initial statutory intervention into this area occurred, with s 9(2) of the European Communities Act 1972, it was unclear whether the decision in *Newborne v Sensolid* had been affected. The position was, however, clarified to some extent by the Court of Appeal in *Phonogram v Lane*.[36] In this case which concerned contracts paid in connection with the formation of a company to manage a pop group, a contract had been signed by the agent 'for and on behalf of Fragile Management Ltd'.

---

35 [1953] 1 All ER 708.
36 [1981] 3 All ER 182.

Applying the European provision, the Court of Appeal confirmed that the agent was liable personally on this contract. They also took the opportunity, however, to indicate disapproval of excessively technical analysis of the precise wording used in transactions of this kind. The view was taken that the court should primarily try to give effect to the intention of the legislation, and only depart from this where the parties had clearly indicated an intention to contract on some other basis. In coming to this conclusion, the court criticised the decision in *Newborne v Sensolid*, to the extent that it was based on a 'narrow point as to the way in which the contract was signed'.[37]

The consequence of this decision is, therefore, that any 'agreement to the contrary' must be very clearly stated in order to be given effect. Although, however, the court disapproved of *Newborne v Sensolid*, it must be noted that *Phonogram v Lane* was concerned with the agent's liability rather than the agent's power to enforce. To that extent, its view of *Newborne v Sensolid* is strictly *obiter*. Nevertheless, the overall approach is one which shows a desire to avoid excessively detailed and technical interpretation of either the statute or the language used as between the parties. It seems likely, therefore, that Bowstead is justified in suggesting that s 36(4) of the Companies Act 1985 is likely to be interpreted as giving the agent the power to enforce, as well as imposing liability on the agent.[38]

The approach in this area (ie pre-incorporation contracts relating to companies) may be seen as one that favours the third party. If the purported agent wants to avoid liability, then positive steps must be taken to achieve this. The presumption will otherwise be that the agent is personally liable. The position is slightly different, however, in relation to contracts purported to be made on behalf of unincorporated associations, such as clubs, societies or voluntary organisations. Such an association does not, by definition, constitute a separate legal person. It cannot make contracts, nor sue or be sued on them.[39] The rights and liabilities of a person purporting to act as agent for such an association seem to depend on the knowledge of the third party. In *Steele v Gourley*[40] the issue was a contract to supply goods to a club. It was held that if the third party was looking to the club alone for payment, then the members of the committee which had authorised the contract were not personally liable. If, however, the third party was throughout looking to the

---

[37] *Ibid, per* Oliver LJ, at p 188.

[38] *Op cit*, p 472

[39] Note, however, the slightly anomalous position of a registered trade union, which by virtue of s 10(1) of the Trade Union and Labour Relations (Consolidation) Act 1992 can sue or be sued in its own name.

[40] (1887) 3 TLR 772.

committee for payment, then they would be personally liable. The knowledge and state of mind of the third party thus becomes the determining factor.[41] Those dealing with, or on behalf of, such unincorporated associations should, therefore, make sure that the expectations as regards liability and payment are made absolutely clear prior to entering into any contract.

LIABILITY ON A COLLATERAL CONTRACT

It is quite possible for an agent to be liable on a collateral contract with the third party. For example, the agent may in pre-contractual negotiations make promises outside their authority which induced the third party to enter into the contract with the principal. There are obviously close links here with the agent's liability for misrepresentations, discussed below.

BREACH OF THE IMPLIED WARRANTY OF AUTHORITY

Closely allied to the concept of the collateral contract is the action for breach of the implied warranty of authority. This arises where an agent is taken to have represented to a third party that he has authority from a principal, when in fact no such authority has been given. Such a warranty will always arise where the agent acts for a disclosed principal. A false statement of this kind may, if fraudulent, give rise to an action for deceit, or if negligent, one under *Hedley Byrne v Heller*,[42] or, possibly, the Misrepresentation Act 1967. If, however, it is entirely innocent, the third party may be able to rescind any resulting contract,[43] but the primary remedy will be that for breach of the implied warranty. This action is, in fact, available for any false statement as to authority, whether fraudulent, negligent or innocent. The broader remedies available, however, for fraudulent or negligent statements mean that the most likely use of the action for breach of the implied warranty is going to be in relation to innocent statements of this kind.

The availability of the remedy for breach of this warranty was established in *Collen v Wright*.[44] W was a land agent who thought that he had G's authority to lease some of G's property, though in fact he did

---

[41] See also *Jones v Hope* (1880) 3 TLR 247.

[42] [1963] 2 All ER 575.

[43] But note the bars to rescission, ie affirmation, lapse of time, impossibility of restitution.

[44] (1857) 8 E&B 647.

not. W purported to lease the property to C. C sued G for specific performance. When this action failed, C sued W. It was held that C was entitled to recover for breach of the implied warranty of authority. He was awarded damages to cover the cost of work he had done on the land, and the costs of the action against G.

As will be seen from this case, the remedies will be different from those available in an action under the contract itself. In *Collen v Wright* the plaintiff was seeking what would nowadays be called damages based on the 'reliance' interest. These could never have been available from G. If, on the other hand, the plaintiff is seeking to recover the expectation interest, ie the benefits that would have come from the contract if it had been made with authority, it will only be possible to recover what could have been obtained in an action against the purported principal. Thus if, for example, the principal is insolvent, the plaintiff may recover very little.

The fact that liability under this head is not dependent on deceit or negligence can lead to somewhat harsh results in certain circumstances. In *Yonge v Toynbee*,[45] for example, a solicitor was held liable for breach of the warranty where he continued to act for a client who, unknown to the solicitor, had been certified as a lunatic. This certification automatically terminated the solicitor's authority. He was, therefore, albeit unknowingly, acting in breach of the implied warranty of authority in continuing to act for his client. This rather strict rule does not, however, apply to an agent acting under a power of attorney. Section 5(1) of the Powers of Attorney Act 1971 provides that:

> A donee of a power of attorney who acts in pursuance of the power at a time when it has been revoked shall not, by reason of the revocation, incur any liability (either to the donor or to any other person) if at the time he did not know that the power had been revoked.

LIABILITY IN TORT

Where an agent commits a tort in connection with some activity authorised by the principal, the principal is likely to be vicariously liable. Unlike the standard position in relation to contractual liability, however, the fact that the principal is liable does not absolve the agent from liability. The normal position will be that the agent (like an employee) is also personally liable for the tortious act.[46] The agent who, in the course

---

45 [1910] 1 KB 215.
46 Eg *Adler v Dickson* [1955] 1 QB 158.

of the agency, commits an assault, or negligently causes damage to a third party's property, for example, can be sued for this. Often, therefore, the victim of the tortious act will have the possibility of suing either the principal, or the agent, or both. The consequences of this are considered, below on p 144. There are, however, some particular situations where the liability of the agent needs to be considered in more detail.

Conversion

The agent who, on the instructions of a principal, deals with goods belonging to someone other than the principal, knowing that this is usurping the rights of the true owner, will commit the tort of conversion. It seems, however, that an innocent agent who deals with goods *in the agent's possession*, eg by selling them, or refusing to hand them over to the true owner, will also commit the tort, even if acting in the reasonable, but mistaken, belief that the goods belong to the principal.[47] A number of the cases in this area concern auctioneers. Thus in *Cochrane v Rymill*[48] the principal had delivered to an auctioneer certain cabs which, unknown to the auctioneer, he had merely hired from a third party. The auctioneer sold the cabs, and, despite his ignorance of the situation, was held liable to the third party in conversion. The agent who refuses to hand over goods until the true position has been clarified, however, does not commit the tort.[49]

Defamation

The agent who passes on an untrue defamatory statement emanating from the principal will be jointly liable to the injured party in libel (or, if the statement is spoken, slander). The tort is one of strict liability, in the sense that there is no requirement to prove that the publisher of the statement was aware that it was untrue, or might be taken to apply to the plaintiff. The law in this area requires those who publish defamatory material to take special care. The agent will, however, be able to take advantage of all the usual defences, such as fair comment, qualified privilege, or 'unintentional defamation' under s 4 of the Defamation Act 1952. Even if the principal is motivated by malice, and cannot therefore rely on the defence, the agent who acts innocently is allowed to claim its protection.[50] In addition, the agent who can claim to be an 'innocent

---

[47] Eg *Consolidated Co v Curtis & Son* [1892] 1 QB 405.

[48] (1879) 40 LT 744.

[49] *Alexander v Southey* (1821) 5 B&A 247.

[50] *Egger v Viscount Chelmsford* [1964] 3 All ER 406.

distributor' will not be liable.[51] This requires the agent to prove that they were unaware of the defamatory statement (eg if it was contained in a book or magazine distributed by the agent) and had no reason to believe that the publication contained such a statement.[52]

Deceit and negligent misstatement

The position in relation to the principal's liability for these torts has been discussed in Chapter 4.[53] The agent can also be personally liable for them, but the plaintiff will have to prove the relevant elements in relation to the agent. Thus, for deceit, it is necessary that the agent should have the required state of mind, they will not be infected by the principal's knowledge or recklessness as regards the truth or falsity of the statement.[54] For negligent misstatement under *Hedley Byrne v Heller*[55] what is needed is the existence of a duty of care as between the agent and third party, based on the required 'proximity'. Thus in *Smith v Bush*[56] the House of Lords held that a surveyor who carried out a survey of a house on behalf of a building society owed a duty to the purchaser of the house, whom the surveyor was aware would rely on the survey. He was therefore liable for negligent statements in the survey relating to the house. In *Gran Gelato v Richcliff*,[57] however, Nicholls VC counselled caution in finding a duty as between agent and third party:

> There will be cases where it is fair, just and reasonable that there should be such a duty. But, in general, in a case where the principal himself owes a duty of care to the third party, the existence of a further duty of care, owed by the agent to the third party, is not necessary for the protection of the latter. Good reason, therefore, should exist before the law imposes a duty when the agent already owes to his principal a duty which covers the same ground and the principal is responsible to the third party for his agent's shortcomings.[58]

Applying this approach, he did not feel that there was any need to impose a duty as between a solicitor acting for the landlord of a

---

51 *Vizetelly v Mudie's Select Library Ltd* [1900] 2 QB 170.
52 For a full discussion of these defences see, for example, WVH Rogers, *Winfield and Jolowicz on Tort*, 14th edn, Ch 12.
53 Above, p 114.
54 *Armstrong v Strain* [1952] 1 KB 232.
55 [1964] AC 465.
56 [1990] 1 AC 831.
57 [1992] 1 All ER 865.
58 *Ibid*, at p 873.

property, and a prospective lessee, in relation to the answers given to 'inquiries before lease'. The fact the principal may be insolvent, and therefore unable to meet any successful claim, is not in itself a sufficient reason for imposing a duty on the agent.

Two caveats should be noted in relation to this decision. First, it is only a first instance decision. As such, its effect should probably be limited to the situation with which it was directly concerned – ie a solicitor answering inquiries before contract. To the extent that the judgment is expressed in general terms relating to an agent's liability for negligent misstatement, it should be approached with caution. Second, the judgment is only concerned with negligent misstatements. It should not be taken as having any relevance to other types of negligent actions. In *White v Jones*,[59] for example, the House of Lords held that a solicitor who negligently failed to carry out a client's instructions relating to a will owe a duty of care to the disappointed intended beneficiary. Nevertheless, even to this limited extent, *Gran Gelato v Richcliff* does constitute a significant departure from the position whereby in general both principal and agent will be liable for tortious acts of the agent.

Before leaving this area, it should be noted that an agent will not generally have liability for negligent misstatement under s 2(1) of the Misrepresentation Act 1967. This is because the section specifically imposes liability on those who are 'parties' to a contract. The agent is not generally a party and therefore cannot be liable under this provision. This interpretation of the wording of the section was confirmed by Mustill J in *Resolute Maritime Inc v Nippon Kaiji Kyokai*.[60]

Exemption clauses

The contract between a principal and third party may sometimes try to protect the agent, by incorporating provisions purporting to exclude or limit the agent's liability to the third party for torts committed by the agent. In general, such attempts will not be successful. The standard rule, which applies also to employees or independent contractors, in favour of whom such protection may be attempted, as well as to agents, is that since none of these is a party to the contract, the doctrine of privity prevents them from enforcing any benefits purported to be conferred on them by the contract. English law does not recognise the concept of 'vicarious immunity', to balance that of 'vicarious liability'. Such a concept was firmly rejected by the House of Lords in *Scruttons Ltd v Midland Silicones Ltd*.[61]

---

[59] [1995] 1 All ER 691.

[60] [1983] 2 All ER 1.

[61] [1962] AC 446.

Over the past 30 years there have been various attempts to try to enable English law to take account of the commercial reality that the parties to a complex business contract are often willing to extend protection to those who are not parties, and that little purpose is served by thwarting such intentions.[62] Two approaches have proved successful. The first, recognised in *New Zealand Shipping Company v Satterthwaite (The Eurymedon)*,[63] involved treating the independent contractor in this case as authorising the party to the contract to make a collateral contract on its behalf. The terms of this collateral contract were that the independent contractor would gain the benefit of the exemption clause, in return for performing certain actions relevant to the contract (in this case, unloading goods). The contracting party was thus deemed to be acting as 'agent' for the independent contractor. To apply this approach to the situations we are considering would be to turn the agency relationships on their head. The principal would have to be treated as acting as 'agent' for the agent, who would for these purposes become the 'principal'. It seems unlikely that the courts would be prepared to assent to such a twisting of the true position, simply in order to extend the scope of an exclusion clause. It may well be, therefore, that the *Satterthwaite* approach, while useful for independent contractors, is inappropriate, and unavailable, for agents.

The second way in which a person not party to the contract has effectively been granted the benefit of an exclusion clause purporting to protect them from liability in negligence, is via a modification of the duty of care. In *Southern Water Authority v Carey*[64] sub-contractors were held not to have a duty towards the plaintiff, because the existence of the exclusion clause in the plaintiff's contract with the main contractor precluded such a duty from arising. The same approach was taken in *Norwich City Council v Harvey*.[65] There seems no reason why this should not also, in appropriate circumstances, operate to the benefit of an agent. It may also be felt to have some resonance with the views of Nicholls VC in *Gran Gelato v Richcliff*[66] (discussed in the previous section), to the effect that the personal liability of an agent in negligence should be controlled by restricting the scope of the duty of care.

---

[62] The position is different where one of the parties is a 'consumer', on whom the exclusion clause may have been 'imposed': cf *Adler v Dickson* [1955] 1 QB 158.

[63] [1974] 1 All ER 1015.

[64] [1985] 2 All ER 1077.

[65] [1989] 1 All ER 1180.

[66] [1992] 1 All ER 865.

BOTH PRINCIPAL AND AGENT LIABLE

In some situations, as we have seen, a third party may be in a position where either agent or principal can be sued. Can the third party sue both? If so, how are the liabilities to be divided? The position differs according to whether the action is contractual or tortious, and so the two situations must be considered separately.

Contract

The starting point is that in a contract there is only one set of obligations. Either principal or agent may be liable for breach of these, but not both. This is sometimes referred to as the doctrine of 'merger'. At what stage, if any, then, does the third party have to decide which of the two is going to be made the subject of legal action? Obviously, the third party will not be allowed to enforce a judgment against both. This would give rise to double recovery, and run contrary to the doctrine of merger. But what if the third party has obtained judgment against one of the two, but the selected defendant is unable to pay? Can the third party switch the attack to the other potential defendant? If not, at what earlier stage must a choice be made?

The rules in this area are not very certain but it seems that:

- If judgment has been obtained against either principal or agent, this debars action against the other, even if the judgment remains unsatisfied. This follows from the doctrine of merger, and the idea that although two parties are involved (principal and agent) there is only one legal obligation.[67]

- In other situations it seems that if the third party can be said to have 'elected' to sue either the principal or agent, then any action against the other party will be barred. The difficulty remains in deciding exactly what constitutes such an election.

The matter was considered in some detail in *Clarkson Booker Ltd v Andjel*.[68] The plaintiff had supplied the defendant with airline tickets for which the defendant had failed to pay. The plaintiff discovered that the defendant had acted as agent for P&M Ltd. The plaintiff pressed both the defendant and P&M Ltd for payment. Eventually a writ was issued against P&M. The plaintiff then discovered that the firm was insolvent, and tried to bring an action against the defendant. The defendant

---

[67] *Cf* the principle of *res judicata*.
[68] [1964] 3 All ER 260.

claimed that the issue of the first writ constituted an election, thereby barring any action against him. The Court of Appeal ruled that the question of whether or not there had been an election was a question of fact rather than law. Although it was felt that the institution of legal proceedings raises a *prima facie* case of election, before the court would give effect to this, it had to be clear that the third party had full knowledge of all relevant facts, and that the alleged election was a 'truly unequivocal act'.[69] Applying this to the facts of the case, it might have been argued that, since the plaintiff did not know at the time of the issue of the writ that P&M were insolvent, he was not thus in possession of all relevant facts, and the issue of the writ was therefore not an election. Willmer LJ, however, appears to equate the 'relevant facts' in this situation with the plaintiff's rights against the agent: 'it cannot be suggested that when the plaintiffs made their decision to institute proceedings against [P&M] they were in any way ignorant of their rights against the defendant'.[70] Both he and the other members of the Court of Appeal decided the case on the basis that in the circumstances of the case the issue of the writ was nevertheless not a truly unequivocal act. This was in part because the plaintiff's had up until the time of the issue of the writ continued to seek payment from the defendant, as well as from P&M. Issue of a writ against one party where there has been no previous claim against the other (despite knowledge of the possibility) would be much more likely to be considered an election.

This decision, although to some extent helpful, still leaves open the question of what actually constitutes a 'truly unequivocal act'. Since this is a question of fact, it seems that it has to be left to be decided in the light of the particular circumstances of each individual case. This is not, however, very helpful to the third party who has to try and guess who will be the most likely of the two potential defendants to satisfy any legal action taken against them.

The decision in *Clarkson Booker v Andjel* was followed by the Court of Appeal in *Chestertons v Barone*.[71] The question was whether the third party had elected to sue the, originally undisclosed, principal, and was based on the wording of letters sent prior to the issue of a writ. It was held that in exceptional circumstances an election might be shown without legal proceedings being initiated, but that 'the clearest evidence of an election is at least the commencement of proceedings by the plaintiff against one or other of the two relevant parties'.[72]

---

[69] *Per* Willmer LJ at p 266.

[70] *Ibid*.

[71] [1987] 1 EGLR 15.

[72] *Ibid, per* May LJ, at p 17.

The uncertainty in this area has led at least one commentator to argue that there is no need for a separate doctrine of election and that the situations in which it is wrong to allow for joint liability could be satisfactorily dealt with by other concepts, such as *res judicata*, or estoppel.[73] This rejects the doctrine of merger, and would recognise a greater scope for joint and several liability in contract.[74] The argument is perhaps strongest in relation to disclosed principals. Where there is an undisclosed principal whose existence, for example, the third party does not discover until proceedings have been launched against the agent, it would seem wrong to refuse to allow the agent to seek to make the principal liable in place of the agent.

Liability in tort

In contrast with the position in contract, where agent and principal are liable in tort, this is regarded as consisting of separate obligations. Liability is therefore joint and several. The third party does not therefore have to worry about which to sue, other than to take account of any factors which might mean that one of the two can avoid liability (eg under an exemption clause).[75] The issue as to the division of responsibility between the two tortfeasors will be governed by the Civil Liability (Contribution) Act 1978. Section 1(1) allows any person liable in respect of damage suffered by another to recover a contribution from any other person who is also liable in respect of the same damage. The amount of the contribution will be 'such as may be found to be just and equitable'.[76] The contribution cannot be greater, however, than the amount the contributor would have been liable to pay to the plaintiff.[77] Thus, if principal or agent (it is more likely to be the principal) is protected by a contractual provision limiting liability to the third party to a particular sum, then that will be the maximum that can be required by way of a contribution under the 1978 Act.

The Act does not operate in any special way as regards agency arrangements, and any standard tort text should be consulted for a more detailed discussion of its provisions.[78]

---

73 Reynolds, 'Election distributed', 86 LQR 318; cf Bowstead, *op cit*, pp 346–52.

74 With contributions as between principal and agent being dealt with by the Civil Liability (Contribution) Act 1978; discussed below in the section dealing with tort liability.

75 See above, p 142.

76 Section 2(1).

77 Section 2(3).

78 Eg Rogers, W V H *Winfield and Jolowicz on Tort*, 14th edn, pp 627–31.

The provisions of the Act make life easier for the third party considering a tortious action against the principal or agent. There is a strong argument for saying that a similar approach should be adopted in relation to contractual actions, but at the moment there seems no prospect of a change of the law as outlined in the previous section.

CHAPTER 6

TERMINATION OF AGENCY

INTRODUCTION

This chapter is concerned with the various ways in which an agency relationship may be brought to an end. It is important in this context to distinguish between the termination of an agent's authority, and the termination of any contract which may have created that authority. The two may in many cases be co-terminous, but are not necessarily so. In some circumstances authority may be brought to an end, even though the underlying contract still technically subsists. Conversely, as far as a third party is concerned, ostensible authority may continue to operate,[1] despite the termination of any actual authority, and any contract between principal and agent.

The first part of the chapter concentrates on the common law rules that operate in this area. The second part looks at the statutory regulations which apply to 'commercial agents'.[2]

COMMON LAW RULES

Termination by act of the parties

Agreement

In the same way that an agency relationship may be created by agreement, so it is determinable in the same way. If principal and agent both agree that the relationship should come to an end, and the terms on which it should do so, then their intentions will be given effect.

Notice

It is particularly important in relation to notice to make the distinction between the termination of authority, and the termination of a contract. There are certain situations, considered below, where an agent's

---

[1] See Chapter 4, pp 98–103.

[2] Ie under the Commercial Agents (Council Directive) Regulations 1993, SI 1993/3053.

authority is regarded as irrevocable, so that any purported notice of termination can only affect the underlying contract. Conversely, in other cases, notice may be effective to terminate an agent's authority, without necessarily destroying the contract that created it. Generally, however, an agency contract may be terminated by the principal giving notice to the agent. If no period of notice is specified in the contract that created the agency, then reasonable notice should be given (unless the agent is also an employee, when statutory provisions relating to notice will apply).[3] What is reasonable will depend on the circumstances of each case. An example is *Martin-Baker Aircraft v Murison*.[4] The defendant had agreed to act as 'sole selling agent' for the plaintiff's products in North America. The defendant was also required to promote the plaintiffs' products in that area. When the plaintiffs sought to terminate this agreement, the defendant claimed that, in the absence of any breach of contract, this could only be done by mutual consent. McNair J, however, held that the agreement was analogous to an employment contract. It was a commercial relationship based on confidence and trust, and as such was terminable on reasonable notice. The decision as to what constituted reasonable notice had to take account of the circumstances existing at the time the notice was given. On the facts, it was held that 12 months notice was reasonable.

It was probably significant that in this case there were mutual obligations, so that the agreement was clearly 'bilateral'. In an agency arrangement under which the agent receives commission for transactions entered into, but is not *obliged* to do anything particular to further the principal's interests, the agreement will be 'unilateral'. In that case, the normal rules for termination of offers in a unilateral contract will apply. In other words, the 'offer' can generally be withdrawn at any time before acceptance;[5] this means that such an agency agreement is effectively terminable summarily (in the absence of other agreement). This was the view taken in *Motion v Michaud*,[6] which was distinguished in *Martin-Baker v Murison*.[7]

Even if notice is given by the principal which is not in accordance with the above rules, and may, for example, itself constitute a breach of contract, it will nevertheless be effective to terminate the agent's actual authority. An agent who has been told by the principal that their authority has been revoked, is not entitled to bind the principal by any

---

3   Employment Protection Consolidation Act 1978.

4   [1955] 2 QB 556.

5   But *cf Errington v Errington and Woods* [1952] 1 All ER 149; *Daulia Ltd v Four Millbank Nominees* [1978] 2 All ER 557.

6   (1892) 8 TLR 447.

7   See also Bowstead, *op cit*, pp 528–31.

future acts.[8] Third parties may still be able to rely on ostensible authority. If, however, the notice does constitute a breach of contract, it will almost certainly give the agent a right of action against the principal on this basis.

The above discussion relates to notice given by the principal. It is also possible for the agent to renounce authority. Bowstead asserts that such renunciation is only effective to terminate authority if it is accepted by the principal.[9] No cases are cited in support of this proposition, but it seems right in principle. The power to grant authority lies with the principal, not with the agent; the decision whether the authority terminates or not should thus also lie with the principal. It is unlikely, however, that the point will have much practical significance. Generally the principal will accept an agent's renunciation, and even if it is not accepted, it seems unlikely that the agent in such a situation would act in such a way as to continue to exercise the renounced authority.

As noted above, in some situations, an agent's authority is said to be 'irrevocable'. Under the common law, an irrevocable authority can arise where it is given in order to protect an agent's interest. Thus, if, as in *Gaussen v Morton*,[10] the principal owes money to the agent, and gives the agent a power of attorney to sell land with the intention that the proceeds will be used to pay off the debt, the power cannot be revoked. In this case, the authority was granted by deed, but the same will apply where the agreement to give the authority is simply supported by consideration, as long as at the time the authority was given the intention was that it would be used to protect the agent's interest. If the agent receives the principal's property with a view to sale, and then subsequently makes advances to the principal, the power to sell the property is not irrevocable.[11] Note that what is required is not an agreement that the authority will be irrevocable, but simply an agreement to protect the agent's interest, supported by valuable consideration. It follows from this that the mere existence of an agent's lien over the principal's property[12] does not in itself make the agent's authority irrevocable.

The common law approach to irrevocability has been given statutory recognition in respect of powers of attorney by s 4(1) of the Powers of Attorney Act 1971. This states that:

---

8   *Frith v Frith* [1906] AC 254.
9   *Op cit*, pp 508–9.
10 (1830) 10 B&C 731.
11 *Smart v Sandars* (1848) 5 CB 895.
12 See Chapter 3, p 80.

Where a power of attorney is expressed to be irrevocable and is given to secure –

(a) a proprietary interest of the donee of the power; or

(b) the performance of an obligation owed to the donee,

then, so long as the donee has that interest or the obligation remains undischarged, the power shall not be revoked –

(i) by the donor, without the consent of the donee; or

(ii) by the death, incapacity or bankruptcy of the donor or, if the donor is a body corporate, by its winding up or dissolution.

The statute requires an express statement of irrevocability, whereas the common law only requires an express intention to protect the agent's interest. Second, the reference in 4(1)(b) to 'the performance of an obligation owed to the donee' appears to have the potential to allow irrevocability to operate in a wider range of situations than is covered by the common law. Otherwise, however, the statute follows the common law which also, where irrevocability applies, prevents death, incapacity or bankruptcy from having their normal effects of terminating an agent's authority. Section 5(3) gives protection to a third party dealing with an agent who appears to be acting under an irrevocable power of attorney. The third party will not be treated as having notice of any revocation of the power, unless the third party knows that it has been revoked by the donor with the consent of the donee. Where the power is an enduring power of attorney which by virtue of s 7(1) of the Enduring Powers of Attorney Act 1985 cannot be revoked by the donor without the approval of the court, the third party will not be taken to have knowledge of the revocation unless they know that the court has confirmed this.[13]

Operation of law

Normal termination

The nature of the agency arrangement itself may result in it coming to an end at a particular time. For example, if an agent is employed to carry out a particular transaction, the relationship will terminate once that transaction has been completed. Thus, in *Blackburn v Scholes*[14] a broker who had sold goods as agreed had no authority to agree to a subsequent alteration of the terms. His actual authority had terminated with the sale (though ostensible authority might have continued).

---

13 Enduring Powers of Attorney Act 1985, s 9(5).
14 (1810) 2 Camp 341.

Similarly, if the agency is from the outset expressed to last for a specified period, authority will automatically cease at the end of the period. A stockbroker's authority, for example, may, in the absence of other agreement, be taken to cease at the end of the current account.[15]

Subsequent events

Physical

The occurrence of certain events will automatically bring the agent's authority to an end. For example, if an agent is employed to sell a particular house which then burns down, the agency will be terminated. If the agency results from a contract, then in such a situation the contract would also be regarded as being frustrated. A similar result will follow if either the principal or agent dies. Thus in *Blades v Free*[16] a man had allowed a woman with whom he had once cohabited to order goods to his account. His death, however, automatically terminated her authority. His estate was not even bound by contracts made before the woman became aware of his death. Since agency is a fiduciary relationship, the personalities of the parties involved are important. It would not generally be acceptable for the estate of either the principal or agent simply to take over the relationship. It may be possible for transactions entered into in ignorance of the death to be ratified, however,[17] and in *Blades v Free* it was suggested that the estate might be bound if the principal has expressly contracted for goods to be supplied (eg to his widow) after his death.

If either party acts in a way that is inconsistent with the continuance of the agency, this may mean that authority is terminated. Particular problems can arise where the principal withdraws from the area of activity in which the agent has been employed. It seems that such withdrawal will automatically terminate the agent's authority, as in *Rhodes v Forwood*[18] where the agent was employed to sell coal, but the principal sold the colliery. Moreover, the agent will not be able to claim any compensation for such termination, unless the contract with the principal expressly, or possibly impliedly, committed the principal to the agency arrangement for a particular length of time. In *Turner v Goldsmith*[19] the agent successfully argued a right to compensation on the basis that the agency to sell the principal's shirts was expressly stated to

---

15   *Lawford & Co v Harris* (1896) 12 TLR 275.
16   (1829) 9 B & C 167; see also *Campanari v Woodburn* (1854) 15 CB 400.
17   *Foster v Bates* (1843) 12 MLW 226.
18   (1876) 1 App Cas 256.
19   [1891] 1 QB 544.

last five years, and was not terminated by the fact that the principal's factory was burned down, and the principal went out of business. There are few cases, however, where the agent has been able to argue successfully for an *implied* term of this kind, the courts applying here, as elsewhere in the law of contract,[20] a strict approach to such implication.[21] The case law in this area is, however, primarily about compensation, and there does not seem to be any dispute as regards the general rule that the principal's withdrawal will terminate the agent's actual authority. As far as compensation is concerned, an interesting comparison can be withdrawn with the regime which now applies to 'commercial agents', and which is discussed below.[22]

Legal

Events that affect legal capacity will generally terminate an agency relationship. Thus if, for example, the principal goes into liquidation (if a company) or becomes bankrupt (if an individual), then the agency will automatically terminate. The same will generally be true if it is the agent who loses capacity. Similarly, external events which render the performance of the agency illegal will have a similar effect. If, for example, the purpose of the agency was to trade in certain items (eg ivory), and the government bans such trade, then this would terminate the agent's authority and probably frustrate any underlying contract. Another comparable situation would be if one of the parties, as a result of a declaration of war, becomes an enemy alien. This again would render any transactions illegal, terminate the agent's authority, and frustrate any contract between principal and agent.

EFFECTS OF TERMINATION

On principal and agent

As noted at the start of this chapter, it is important to distinguish between the termination of the agency itself, where the primary effect relates to the agent's actual authority, and the termination of any underlying contract. As far as the agent's actual authority is concerned, where an agency relationship terminates, rights vested at the time of termination will subsist, but no new rights can be created. Whether the

---

[20] Eg *The Moorcock* (1889) 14 PD 64; *Liverpool City Council v Irwin* [1977] AC 236.

[21] See eg *French Ltd v Leeston Shipping Co Ltd* [1922] 1 AC 451.

[22] At p 163.

agent is able to claim commission for actions taken prior to the termination will largely depend on a careful analysis of the agreement governing the agency, of the kind discussed in Chapter 3.[23] If, for example, the agent is required to find 'ready, willing and able' purchasers, and has done so at the point when the principal revokes authority, commission may well be claimable even if the transactions themselves are aborted. If, on the other hand, commission is only payable on 'sales', then work done towards a sale, which does not take place because the agency is terminated, will not lead to any entitlement on the part of the agent.

As far as an agent acting on the basis of a power of attorney is concerned, s 5(1) of the Powers of Attorney Act 1971 provides that the agent will incur no liability to the donor, or anyone else, as a result of actions taken without knowledge of any revocation of the power.

Do any of the agent's fiduciary duties towards the principal survive termination of the agency relationship? This issue was considered by Colman J in *Yasuda Fire Insurance v Marine Fire Insurance*,[24] where he also addressed the issue of the survival of the contract beyond termination of authority. The defendants had a contract with the plaintiffs under which they, the defendants, acted as underwriting agents. The contract expressly allowed the plaintiffs, as principals, access to books and records kept by the defendants. The plaintiffs on several occasions sought access to the defendant's computer records, but this was refused on the basis that the computer records also contained information about other business which the defendants contracted with other principals, and this was confidential. The plaintiffs terminated the agency agreement on the basis that the defendants had committed a repudiatory breach. The defendants in their turn claimed that the plaintiffs' termination was in itself a repudiatory breach. The plaintiffs continued to seek access to the defendants' records. This was in order for them to continue to manage the business which the defendants had obtained for them prior to the termination. The defendants alleged that the termination of the agency agreement had also terminated the right of inspection given by the contract. Colman J found for the plaintiffs on two bases. He found first that there was a general duty on an agent to provide a principal with information, irrespective of any contractual provision, because:

> the agent has been entrusted with the authority to bind the principal to transactions with third parties and the principal is entitled to know what his personal contractual rights and duties are in relation

---

[23] Above, p 72.
[24] [1995] 3 All ER 211.

to those third parties as well as what he is entitled to receive by way of payment from the agent.[25]

Since the purpose of this duty is backward-looking, to enable the principal to check on what *has been done* in the principal's name, there is no reason why it should cease to exist on the termination of authority, at least insofar as it relates to transactions entered into prior to such termination.[26] On this basis, the plaintiffs were entitled to succeed in their action.

Turning then to the contract, the defendants had relied on the statements by Lord Diplock in *Photo Production Ltd v Securicor Transport Ltd*[27] to the effect that an accepted repudiatory breach brings to an end the 'primary obligations' under a contract, though 'secondary' obligations, such as the right to damages, or to go to arbitration, may then arise. The defendants in the present case argued that the rights to information given in the contract were primary obligations, and so should be regarded as having ceased to exist on termination. Colman J rejected this analysis. He relied on the statements of the House of Lords in *Heyman v Darwins Ltd*[28] as to the effect of an arbitration clause, coming to the conclusion that these statements indicated that:

> the survival of the arbitration clause in the face of an accepted repudiation is attributable to its having a contractual function ancillary to the subject matter of the contract, namely the resolution of disputes as to the parties' rights and obligations attributable to pre-existing events.[29]

The essential characteristic, in Colman J's view, was the ancillary nature of the clause, not the fact that it only arose following breach of a primary obligation. Applying this approach to the present case, his view was that the inspection obligations contained in the contract were wholly ancillary to the subject matter of the agency agreements. They were not, therefore, primary obligations which terminated with the contract. On this ground again, therefore, he held that the plaintiffs succeeded.

Finally, he ruled that the fact that it would be difficult for the defendants to provide access to their computer records without disclosing other confidential information was effectively their problem: 'It is not open to the defendants to rely on the inseparability of irrelevant

---

25 *Ibid*, at p 219.
26 *Ibid*, at p 220.
27 [1980] 1 All ER 556, at p 566–7.
28 [1942] 1 All ER 337.
29 [1995] 3 All ER 211, at p 224.

material as a basis for declining to permit inspection, extraction and copying of relevant material'.[30]

Although only a first instance decision, this case is important in establishing that an agent's duties may continue beyond termination of authority, whether or not they are based on contract. Each situation will require careful analysis, however, to determine when this will occur.

One situation where it is generally accepted that obligations may survive the ending of a contract is in relation to clauses that attempt to restrict an agent's activities after ceasing to work for a particular principal. The rules that apply here are the same as apply generally in contract law. That is, such attempted restrictions are *prima facie* void as being in restraint of trade.[31] They may be effective, however, if the principal has a legitimate interest to protect, and the restraint is no wider than is reasonable to protect that interest.[32] In relation to a principal, legitimate interests are likely to be the same as apply to an employer. That is, the agent may have had access to trade secrets or commercial information which would be useful to another principal, or may have built up relationships with third parties, which would mean that they would be likely to follow the agent if they transferred allegiance to a new principal. Any restraint, to be valid, will have to be reasonable as regards time, scope and geographical area.

All these matters have to be determined in the light of the circumstances of the particular case, but generally, the courts have only been prepared to allow short periods of restriction eg one or two years. As regards scope, the restriction must only relate to the area of the principal's business with which the agent has been involved.[33] Geographical area will similarly be required to be related to the agent's activities while working for the principal. Assuming the restrictions are reasonable, the principal will be able to obtain an injunction to restrain the agent from breaking its terms. A breach in the absence of an injunction will simply be a breach of contract, compensatable in the normal way. Particular rules now apply in this area as regards 'commercial agents', and these are discussed below.[34]

---

30 *Ibid*, at p 225.

31 *Nordenfelt v Maxin Nordenfelt* [1894] AC 535.

32 For a general discussion of the law in this area, see eg Stone *Contract Law*, Cavendish, 1994, pp 189–99.

33 Eg *Littlewoods Organisation Ltd v Harris* [1978] 1 All ER 1026.

34 At p 165.

On third party

Where agency is terminated by notice, the agent may continue to bind the principal until the agent has received notice of the termination.[35] This is also the position as regards powers of attorney, by virtue of s 5(1) of the Powers of Attorney Act 1971.[36] Furthermore, s 5(2) of the Act specifically protects the third party who deals with the agent in ignorance of the fact that the power has been revoked. Any transaction is, as far as the third party is concerned, to be regarded as 'as valid as if the power had then been in existence'.

Aside from these statutory interventions, once the *agent* has received notice of revocation, the position of the third party will generally depend on ostensible authority. If it can be said that the principal has held the agent out as having authority, and has not done sufficient to notify the third party of the withdrawal of that representation, the third party will still be able to hold the principal responsible for the agent's actions. The issue of ostensible authority has been fully discussed in Chapter 4.[37] Two further cases can be noted here as examples of the operation of the concept of ostensible authority in a situation of revocation of actual authority by notice. In *Trueman v Loder*,[38] the agent had regularly acted for a principal based in St Petersburgh. The principal notified the agent of the termination of the agency. A third party contracted with the agent, believing him to be acting for the principal, though that was not the agent's intention. It was held that the principal was nevertheless liable on the transaction, the plaintiff having had no notice that a contract made by the agent was no longer to be regarded as being made for the principal. Similarly, in *Curlewis v Birkbeck*,[39] the plaintiff had used a dealer as agent for the sale of some horses. The defendant bought the horses, and paid the dealer, not knowing that the plaintiff had withdrawn the dealer's authority to receive payment. It was held that the defendant was entitled to assume that the dealer had authority to receive payment, unless he had had notice of revocation of such authority. In the absence of this, the payment made to the dealer discharged any obligation owed to the plaintiff. If ostensible authority does not operate to make the principal liable, then the agent will be liable either on any contract entered into with the third party, or for breach of the implied warranty of authority.[40]

---

[34] At p 000.

[35] *Re Oriental Bank Corp, ex p Guillemin* (1884) 28 Ch 639.

[36] See p 155.

[37] At p 98.

[38] (1840) 11 Ad&E 539.

[39] (1863) 3 F&F 893.

[40] See Chapter 5, p 138.

The above rules apply where the agency is terminated by notice. The position is different if the reason for termination is either the death or insanity of the principal. Where the principal dies, as we have seen from *Blades v Free*,[41] the agent's authority terminates immediately, even before the agent is aware of the death. Moreover, it is not thought appropriate here that ostensible authority should operate to bind the principal's estate. In this situation, therefore, the third party is left to seek recourse against the agent alone.

The position is similar in some respects in relation to the insanity of the principal. In discussing this method of termination earlier it was noted that it took immediate effect, and that in *Yonge v Toynbee* the agent was liable for breach of the implied warranty of authority where the principal had become certifiably insane, even though the agent was unaware of this. A further case dealing with these issues is *Drew v Nunn*.[42] The plaintiff was a tradesman. The defendant had given his wife authority to deal with the plaintiff, and pledge his credit. The defendant went insane. His wife, however, continued to order goods from the plaintiff (who was unaware of the defendant's insanity). The defendant then recovered his reason, but refused to pay for goods supplied during his insanity. The Court of Appeal held that the plaintiff could recover from the defendant. Brett LJ held that insanity had terminated the agency between the defendant and his wife, but that the plaintiff could nevertheless recover. The defendant had never revoked the authority given to the wife and:

> where one of two persons both innocent must suffer by the wrongful act of a third person, that person making the representation which, as between the two, was the original cause of the mischief must be the sufferer, and must bear the loss.[43]

As will be seen from this quotation, Brett LJ was basing liability on ostensible authority. This is in conflict with *Yonge v Toynbee*, since there cannot be an action for breach of warranty of authority if there is ostensible authority. The cases may not, however, be irreconcilable, if the other judgments in *Drew v Nunn* are considered. Thus Bramwell LJ said that the defendant was not sufficiently affected by his mental illness to terminate the wife's agency. Cotton LJ appears to lean towards Bramwell's point of view on this issue. On this analysis, *Drew v Nunn* ceases to be an authority on termination by insanity, and is a straightforward case of ostensible authority. *Yonge v Toynbee* would then be the governing authority. Bowstead, however, prefers to regard *Yonge*

---

[41] Above, p 153.
[42] (1879) 4 QBD 661.
[43] At pp 667–8.

v Toynbee as being a case where ostensible authority was not really relevant,[44] so that the position as regards insanity should be the same as in relation to termination by notice (ie the third party can rely on ostensible authority, unless he or she has notice of the insanity).

Where mental incapacity is more than transitory, a power of attorney created in accordance with s 2 of the Enduring Powers of Attorney Act 1985 will provide some protection to those concerned with the principal's affairs. Such a power can be created at any time when the principal is capable of understanding the nature and effect of the power. They do not need to be capable of managing their affairs.[45] Once created, it is not revoked by the subsequent mental incapacity of the principal, but strict limitations will be imposed on the agent's power to act without the approval of the court.[46] A third party dealing with the agent is entitled to assume, however, that the agent is acting properly, and any transaction between them 'shall be as valid as if' the agent were acting within their powers.[47]

COMMERCIAL AGENTS

As we have seen in earlier chapters, certain special rules now apply to agency relationships which involve 'commercial agents', as defined in the Commercial Agents (Council Directive) Regulations 1993.[48] The definition of a commercial agent for these purposes has been discussed in Chapter 1.[49] Part IV of the regulations sets out rules dealing with the conclusion and termination of the agency contract, and the consequences of this. In some cases these provisions can be seen to replace the common law rules; at other times they operate in addition to, or alongside, the common law.

Fixed term agency

Under the common law, where the parties agree that the agency is to operate for a fixed period, the arrangement will automatically terminate on the expiry of that period, unless there is some specific agreement to continue it. By virtue of reg 14, however, a commercial agency contract

---

[44] *Op cit*, at p 524.
[45] *Re K* [1988] 1 All ER 358.
[46] See s 1(1)(b), and s 1(2).
[47] Section 1(3).
[48] SI 1993/3053.
[49] At p 13.

which is for a fixed period will in some circumstances be converted into an agency contract for an indefinite period. This will happen where both parties continue to act as if the arrangement were still in existence after the expiry of the specified period. Thus, if the principal instructs the agent to enter into further transactions, and the agent complies, or if the agent takes further orders from third parties, and the principal accepts these, then the original agency agreement will be deemed to be still subsisting.

This regulation only applies where the original agency agreement was in the form of a contract, but since the regulations in any case only apply to commercial agents who are paid for their services,[50] this is not a very significant limitation.

Where an agency has been converted in this way by virtue of reg 14, it will be terminable by notice, as discussed in the next section.

Termination of commercial agency

The regulations deal with both immediate termination, and termination by notice.

Immediate termination

Regulation 16 preserves any existing statutory or common law rule providing for 'the immediate termination' of an agency contract 'because of the failure of one party to carry out all or part of his obligations under that contract'. This is presumably intended to refer to the rule whereby a repudiatory breach of contract will, if accepted by the innocent party, bring the contract to an end. To the extent, however, that the wording of the regulation gives the impression that the breach of contract will lead to automatic termination, it is misleading. It seems that although at one time there was some authority for the proposition that in certain circumstances a breach of contract could of itself terminate the agreement, at least since the Court of Appeal's decision in the employment law case of *Gunton v Richmond-upon-Thames London Borough Council*[51] it has been accepted that throughout the English law of contract, the rule is that the innocent party always has the option following a breach to decide whether to continue with the contract or, if the breach is sufficiently serious, to treat it as bringing the contract to an end. Prior to the decision in *Gunton* it had, in any case, been suggested

---

[50] Regulation 2(2)(a).
[51] [1980] 3 All ER 577.

by Lloyd J in *Atlantic Underwriting Agencies Limited and David Gale (Underwriting) Ltd v Compagniadi Assicurazionedi Milano SpA*[52] that this should be the approach to contracts between principal and agent. More recently it was accepted by Colman J in *Yasuda Fire Insurance v Orion Marine Insurance*[53] that a repudiatory breach had to be accepted before it was effective to bring an agency contract to an end. No doubt, however, despite the infelicity of the wording, the regulation will be taken simply to give recognition to the common law rule as it applies to breaches of contract entitling the innocent party to treat the contract as at an end.

Regulation 16(b) similarly provides for the continued operation of any enactment or rule of law providing for immediate termination 'where exceptional circumstances arise'. This presumably has the effect of preserving the application of the doctrine of frustration to contracts creating a commercial agency relationship. The language of immediate termination is more appropriate here, because the frustrating event will operate automatically to discharge the parties from their obligations. It must, however, be remembered that it is only future obligations which are discharged. Any obligations which have arisen prior to the frustrating event will subsist.[54]

Termination by notice

Where a commercial agency operates for an indefinite period, either because it was created in that form, or where a fixed period agency has been converted to an indefinite one by virtue of reg 14 (discussed above), reg 15 prescribes periods of notice for termination. The periods prescribed are minima. The parties themselves may agree on longer periods of notice, subject to the proviso that the principal must always be required to give at least as much notice as the agent in any particular situation.[55] The periods of notice set out in the regulation are related to the length of time for which the agency agreement has been in existence. For these purposes, where a fixed period agency has been converted to an indefinite agency, the fixed period is to be taken into account in calculating the length of the agency agreement for the purposes of determining the minimum requirements as to notice.[56]

The minimum periods of notice set out in reg 15(2) are one month during the first year of the contract; two months during the second year;

---

[52] [1979] 2 Lloyd's Rep 240.
[53] [1995] 3 All ER 211.
[54] See eg the comments of Lord Porter in *Heyman v Darwins Ltd* [1942] 1 All ER 337, at p 361.
[55] Regulation 15 (3).
[56] Regulation 15 (5).

and three months from the start of the third year onwards. Unless the parties agree otherwise, the end of any period of notice given must coincide with the end of a calendar month.[57]

Consequences of termination

Indemnity or compensation

Regulation 17 contains provisions whereby an agent is entitled to receive either compensation, or to be indemnified, in relation to losses, following the termination of the agency contract. This includes termination resulting from the death of the agent, where the compensation or indemnity may be claimed by the deceased's estate.[58] The parties may not alter these provisions to the detriment of the agent, though they may, presumably, agree a more beneficial arrangement.[59] In certain situations, however, specified in reg 18, the agent will lose the right to claim an indemnity or compensation.

There are three situations where this will apply. First, not surprisingly, if the agent has committed a repudiatory breach of contract, and the principal has terminated the agency because of this, the agent will not be able to make any claim under reg 17. Second, if the agent takes the initiative in terminating the agreement, this again will generally remove the right to indemnity or compensation. The right will not be lost, however, even where the agent has terminated the agreement, if the basis for the termination is one of the circumstances specified in reg 18(b). These are that the termination is justified 'by circumstances attributable to the principal', or because the age, infirmity or illness of the agent means that the agent cannot reasonably be required to continue to act. The former provision is presumably mainly concerned with a situation where the principal is in breach of contract. It is not clear whether it is intended to have any wider scope. It probably is, because otherwise there is no reason why the regulation should not have specifically referred to breach by the principal. It is difficult to see, however, what other circumstances would justify termination. The latter part of this provision, dealing with the agent's age, etc would under the common law be more usually dealt with by the doctrine of frustration. The scope of this provision is wider, however, in that it operates where the agent simply acts reasonably in terminating the agreement, rather than simply where it is impossible for the agent to continue to perform the contract. Where this provision applies, the compensation and

---

57 Regulation 15 (4).
58 Regulation 17 (8).
59 Regulation 19.

indemnity provisions in reg 18 will operate in place of the normal rules relating to frustration.

The final grounds for excluding the provisions of reg 17 are that the agent has with the agreement of the principal assigned all rights and duties under the agency contract to another person. The agency as between the original principal and agent has thereby terminated, but it is obviously not a situation where the agent should be entitled to seek compensation.

The arrangement of the provisions in reg 17 are slightly odd, in that it deals first with indemnity and then with compensation. Regulation 17(2) makes it clear, however, that the normal expectation will be for compensation. Indemnity will only be available where the agency contract specifically provides for this. For this reason, compensation will be dealt with first here, and then indemnity.

Regulation 17(6) establishes the basic position that the agent is entitled to compensation for 'damage' suffered as a result of the termination of the agency. Regulation 17(7) then goes on to identify some particular circumstances where damage will be deemed to have occurred. This provision is not exclusive, however, and so it will always be possible for the agent to allege other damage, as long as the causal link between the termination of the agency and the damage can be made. The particular circumstances recognised by reg 17(7) are first, where the termination has deprived the agent of commission which 'proper performance' of the agency contract would have brought the agent. The extent of the compensation available under this heading will depend to some extent on the nature of the agency. If it was for one transaction and the effect of the termination is to deprive the agent of commission on that piece of business, the calculation will be relatively straightforward. If, however, the agent is employed in a more general way to engage in the buying and selling of goods on behalf of the principal, the figures will become more speculative. The reference to 'proper performance' envisages a calculation based on the normal expectation of what the agent would have been doing for the remainder of the contract. Further difficulties may arise depending on whether the contract was for a fixed term or indefinite. If it was indefinite, then presumably the period to consider will be the minimum period of notice which could have been given by the principal to terminate the agency in a proper way.

The second type of damage specifically recognised by reg 17(7) is that arising from the agent's costs and expenses incurred in the performance of the agency contract. If the agent has not been able to 'amortize' such costs and expenses, then they will be recoverable as compensation from the principal. The provisions for compensation thus take account of both the agent's 'expectation' and 'reliance' interests. Compensation can be claimed under both headings in appropriate cases.[60]

If the agency contract allows for the payment of an indemnity, then this will be governed by paras (3) and (4) of reg 17. Paragraph (3) identifies the situations where an indemnity will be available. This is where the agent has either brought in new customers, or has significantly increased the volume of the principal's business, and the principal continues to derive 'substantial benefits' from this. The payment of an indemnity must also be 'equitable having regard to all the circumstances'. In particular, account may be taken of the fact that the agent has lost commission on the new business which has been brought in. If circumstances exist where an indemnity is appropriate, the amount is governed by reg 17(4). This limits the amount of the indemnity to a figure based on the agent's average annual earnings over the preceding five years (or over the entire period of the agency if less than five years). The maximum amount of the indemnity will be the equivalent of one year's remuneration.

The award of an indemnity does not prevent the agent from seeking damages.[61] The agent who wishes to claim either an indemnity or compensation must notify the principal within one year of the termination of the agency of the intention to make such a claim.[62]

Restraint of trade

Any attempt to impose a restraint of trade clause on a commercial agent following the termination of the agreement will be subject to the normal common law rules as discussed earlier in this chapter. In addition, however, reg 20 imposes certain specific controls over such clauses. The first requirement is that any restraint of trade clause must be in writing. It will, in practice, be very rare for a clause of this kind not be incorporated into a written contract. Second, the clause must relate to the geographical area covered by the agent. Where the agent is responsible for a group of customers, the clause must relate to this group as well as to the geographical area. The clause must also relate to the kind of goods covered by the agency contract. Both the requirement as regards geographical area, and that relating to the type of goods concerned, mirror the normal rules operating under the common law. The final specific provision contained in reg 20 is that a restraint of trade clause will only be valid for two years after the termination of the agency

---

[60] Regulation 17(7).

[61] Regulation 17(5).

[62] Regulation 17(9).

contract. The common law rule is that the length of time for which a restraint is imposed must be reasonable in the context of the interest of the principal which is being protected. In some situations a restraint of two years might be regarded as too long. The provision in reg 20(2) simply operates as an upper limit.

INDEX